Japan Unveiled

Understanding Japanese Body Culture

DOMINIQUE BUISSON

HACHETTE Illustrated

▲ A samurai using his bow
to write a poem in the earth.
Cover of a 19th-century
manga.

◄◄ The drum-shaped knot
of a married woman's *obi*.

◄◄ Thoughtful young girl, 1915.

The body in Japanese life

In the Western world, the human body only began to acquire its own identity from the Renaissance onwards, when man stopped being part of the Great Whole, the finite world of Divine Creation, and began to dream of his own glory. People recognised that the body had an existence of its own and began to take care of it, to keep it in shape and attribute meaning to it. Now that they were independent, separate from the Nature surrounding them, people could start dreaming of immortality. The Japanese, however, reject this idea of the body's independence. To them it is an offspring of the Shinto gods. It shares their nature and remains part of Nature itself. Every Japanese owes an imperative duty to his or her body. It is seen as a gift from heaven which must be neither modified nor disguised; it is but one among many constituent parts of a world peopled by divinities and, like them, must be constantly protected from defilement. In its naked state, the body recalls its original purity, but once it is clothed it reveals only appearance and illusion.

The Japanese person described in this book is only an imaginary figure and cannot represent all Japanese people. He or she corresponds to an image built up over the decades not only by foreigners in their studies of Japan, but also by the Japanese themselves, who like to see themselves portrayed by Western minds. This has produced a number of clichés: samurai warriors sacrificing their lives for their code of honour, highly skilled geisha, submissive women, craftsmen of genius and enigmatic actors. Since Japan today is largely made up of people who belong to the same social class, have similar jobs and enjoy similar leisure activities, the country can be seen as one big social body which is loath to reveal itself and prefers to play with paradoxes. This body has its own laws, which express or conceal the real body. It also has its dreams, its imaginary body. As a result, the Japanese are acutely aware of being unique and even cultivate the notion that their manner of behaving is so special that it cannot be understood by the rest of the world. For almost three centuries, when the country was isolated from all foreign influences, Japan – no longer able to compare itself with the rest of the world – had no alternative way of evolving than to perfect its own genius, elevating the most minor aspects of everyday life to the level of ideas and art forms. Nor would their collective unconscious permit the slightest lapse from the narcissistic system which they had created: a vast number of rules, obligations and social categorisations were created so that the body could become an act rather than a mere container, a social grace rather than just a form. While people could use their real bodies to express their desires, strength or professional excellence, their

Tattooed men in a garden – all 'engraved' by the same master tattooist.

dress, make-up and range of gestures were ritualised and codified, like artistic principles, to conform to the aesthetic rules that ensured social harmony.

Japanese architecture is part of this harmony. Based on the module of the human body, it manages the space allocated to the body and adjusts this according to its daily needs, without imposing fixed functions upon it. It is entirely devoted to the body and so, for example, it filters excessively bright light through paper windows, uses shade to encourage an intimate atmosphere, gardens to provide relaxing views, and materials to arouse the senses. In theatre or in dance it is the body itself that is presented, performing rituals in its own space. In the tensions between space and time that these movements create, the body becomes an abstraction, a mystery linked to the sacred origins of the Japanese world. It becomes something beyond the human: a perfect double of the gods.

In Japan, the idea of personal beauty began to be accepted after the Second World War. Previously, each class had its own archetypes to which people had to conform. There was no mirror that told the truth, except those that reflected the proprieties or the poetic imagination. In a society deeply influenced by Buddhism, the emotive quality of objects was long considered the basis of all aesthetic clarity. At that time, lack of ostentation, the innate elegance of moderation, and reserve mixed with melancholy were the signs of a typically Japanese way of seeing things – as distinct from the mysteries of Chinese taste. Aristocratic standards of beauty varied from period to period – nobility and gentleness, simplicity and sobriety, pomp and magnificence, theatricality and eroticism, charm and Westernisation – but all the while Japanese women aroused their partners by the fine texture of their skin and their lustrous black hair. The importance given to hair often exceeded that given to clothes or any other form of adornment. The kimono is the other important attribute of beauty, not only for what it conceals or imperceptibly reveals, but also for its own sake. By the gestures it constrains, it reveals the body and makes its absence a presence. Since the beginning of history, the Japanese dressed to indicate their rank or status; nudity had no part in the social conventions. The body itself was considered devoid of interest. In the past, writers were extremely reluctant to describe how bodies really looked, since this was regarded as obscene, and painters did not possess a visual language that could fully depict them. The naked body was nevertheless visible, at baths or among craftsmen and fishermen, as can be seen in prints, but it was regarded as something functional. If it was related to some kind of aesthetic, this was because of its tattoos, which were not intended to make the body beautiful but to express courage or superstition.

The real, visible body can always be seen as a mere witness to the passage of time, according to the rules of Buddhism, and can only act as a medium for vulgar passions. The Japanese revere those Buddhas who give humans the opportunity to transcend their corporeal being. They also venerate nature, which is always accessible even if it is sometimes terrible. This nature on a human scale involves a close relationship with the divinities that give it life, and people express their solidarity through rites connected to the land or by celebrating important moments in people's lives. These occasions allow the body to express itself, frequently with joy and abandon.

It was not until the beginning of the 20th century that writers such as Tanizaki Junichiro brought the body to a peak of sensuality and ambiguity, but it was after the Second World War in particular that the body became an object of temptation, as in the West, and a means of fighting against traditional inhibitions. The Japanese then became keenly interested in the mobile features of European faces, some even going so far as to reject their classic, national idea of beauty as something 'mellow and vague', and resorting to plastic surgery to change the way they looked. Today, the demands of fashion have put Japanese women under even greater pressure to conform to the international standards exhibited on the catwalk and in the 'beauty' press.

Nevertheless, in matters of seduction, the body always knows the value of concealment as a way of making itself more desirable, creating something erotic from its absence. In contrast, bodies that are dramatised – revealing themselves in the way they move, through codes of behaviour and constraints of dress, or through idealised make-up and masks – change their nature. They raise seduction to the level of a creative act. Although, traditionally, nudity is seen but not looked at in Japan, over the centuries the clothed body has become a fabrication, clad in symbols and social codes, both as it exists in the present and in the way it is constantly reinvented. In Japan, concealment is a means of expression, and all human relations hinge on this ambiguity. Social principles and behaviour are all determined by *tatemae*, outside appearances, but what is most important is what remains hidden: the *honne*, or true intentions. Thus, unlike the West, where conventions and codes are seen as constraints, in Japan these same obligations provide a liberating space in which individuals can define themselves. It is also said that more meanings can be conveyed when there is nothing there, but the younger generations have lost the habit of silence: they do not understand, as their elders do, that empty space contains everything and that time is but an illusion. They create their own fictions and reject those of their parents, but sometimes, inadvertently, they discover those of their remote ancestors. Even today, appearance remains a powerful factor in Japanese society, and although many codes have been revised or criticised, outward appearances involving the presence or absence of the body still need to be seen in relation to the past.

Mask of Okame, a woman of the people.

天神

The sacred body

Japan has a dual religious tradition: Shinto, which is indigenous to the islands, and Buddhism, which was imported from China in 552. In these religions, man and nature are inseparably united in a common life force and in their awareness of being, first and foremost, Japanese. Shinto, or 'Way of the gods', is more a collection of beliefs than an organised doctrine. It is made up of spirits in nature and ancestral gods, and also great men who have been given the divine status, and attributes a spiritual essence to all beings in the universe – to the world of humans as well as to those of animals and plants. Shinto reaches out to people in their daily lives and teaches them to live in a pure manner, respecting the seasonal rhythms of the spirits of nature so that they will attract the goodwill of the supernatural powers. Most of these divinities, the *kami*, are simply spectacular natural phenomena which are elevated to a local cult status, or natural elements to which a spiritual power is attributed. Other *kami*, such as Amaterasu, the sun goddess, ancestor of the Japanese imperial line, or Kono-hana-Sakuya hime, the princess of Mount Fuji, occupy a place that makes them symbolic of Japan itself. In Shinto there is no ethic, no precept that must be followed, except to observe purification rites, appease the *kami* by means of offerings and to 'follow the way of one's heart'. It is a religion without morality and with no explicit concept of an afterlife. This simplicity explains the Japanese liking for raw materials, for wooded spaces free of any blemish and for the clear water of streams. White – symbolising the gods' descent to earth – is the hue that represents this purity, as seen in the small paper strips attached to sacred cords, the robes worn by priests and even the sacred horse, messenger of the *kami*, which must be an albino. For religious robes, the white can be either that of raw silk or 'white' silk, bleached with straw ash so that it never oxidises or yellows with the passage of time.

According to Shinto religion, man is obliged to take care of his body to achieve the harmony of the world. It is imperative, therefore, that pollution of any kind be removed from it. This uniquely Japanese concept of ritual purity and impurity, known as *kegare*, was associated in ancient times with the idea of crime or sin. Apart from lack of cleanliness, the commonest form of defilement was contact with death, but illness, menstruation, wounds, plundering of crops, incest and arson were also considered *kegare*. Since impurities could be transmitted from one person to another, it was necessary to purify oneself by means of the *misogi*, a purification rite using water that

Monk at the Senso-ji temple in Tokyo beats a drum while officiating at a service of the *tendai* sect. He is wearing the *kesa*, a priestly garment that symbolises Buddhism.

the gods themselves practised during their time on the High Plains of the heavens. Those who took part in this rite went to a retreat where they cooked their own meals, so that these might not be defiled by the impure hands of women, and avoided pronouncing any word containing the sound *shi*, meaning death. Today, during private purification ceremonies, for example those linked to contact with death, as in the public ceremonies known as *o-harai*, the services of a priest are employed to drive away demons by waving a whip of white paper, the *haraigushi*, over the heads of the participants. Another means of purification is to take the waters in one of Japan's many volcanic springs, which the Japanese today call 'devil's cauldrons' but which the ancients called 'divine waters'. Some springs, known for their supernatural qualities, have been in use since the sixth century.

The Buddhist tradition is more intellectual. It came from the continent – from China – together with writing, statuary, architecture and the art of government. It too does not neglect the body. Five main schools were introduced to Japan one after the other, each with its own character, and these met the expectations of a growing number of faithful. All these sects grew and multiplied: some were civilising forces or encouraged the arts, others set themselves up as tutors to the powerful, or just as simple models for everyday living. The Zen sect came to be emblematic of Japanese religion because formerly it had gathered together warriors to meditate serenely and because it inculcated in them the spirit of restraint and frugality that is still characteristic of the Japanese soul. Although veneration of the Buddha demanded altars gleaming with gold in the shadows of magnificent temples, the Buddhist ethic was above all a quest for neutrality and simplicity. It was essential therefore that the dress of the pilgrim, novice monk and ordained monk conveyed humility through its shape and hue. This applied chiefly to work clothes, since ceremonial clothes were naturally more elaborate.

In Buddhism, the immutable cycle of rebirth demonstrates that everything is ephemeral and illusory. During their life as a human being, a person has only an anecdotal, limited form of existence, but the origin of suffering lies in the very desire for that existence. Consequently, to escape from the prison of passions and ignorance, we need to kill this desire for existence that lies within us to achieve enlightenment, and try to lose ourselves in *satori*. Thus Buddhism, a philosophy of impermanence, leads the Japanese to appreciate what is most ephemeral and changeable in a landscape: 'the fleeting nuances of things, the movement of clouds, the light of the setting sun in rainy weather, the reflections of moonbeams'[1]. It is probably for these reasons, as well as for its essential meaning, that pilgrimage can be considered one of the most typically Japanese of pleasures, the religious aspect adding mystery and depth to the beauty of nature.

In its relationship with the sacred, the Japanese body adds to, rather than opposes, the principles of these two great religions. Japanese people who do not especially like the idea of an absolute religious dogma, generally choose to be born Shinto and to die as Buddhists. Although important rites of passage are sanctified by the *kami*, death remains the province of Buddhism. Incorporation into the great rhythms of nature, particularly for Shinto, and the unavoidable attachment to human passions, required by Buddhism, create the need for a certain number of purification rites for the body and soul. From childhood onwards, the Japanese is conditioned by certain modes of behaviour derived directly from religion, the most important being the daily ritual of a bath, the evocation of a fundamental episode in the life of the *kami* and the practice of the arts of ceremony, such as the tea ceremony, originally conceived purely for the benefit of Buddhist deities.

Both religions subject the body to severe tests. The Shinto rite of *mizugori* was formerly held in a freezing river, in early January, by young people who needed to toughen their soul as much as their spirit before carrying the divinity's sacred palanquin. Today, the equivalents of this *misogi* are the meditation under a waterfall in winter practised by the members of certain esoteric Buddhist sects, and the *kan-mairi* of the Nichiren sect's faithful, which usually lasts 30 days during winter. Every night they must go from temple to temple, barefoot and wearing only a loincloth, to take an icy shower. Physical strength is still needed during certain festivals, such as the *hakada matsuri*, in which dozens of half-naked young people test their skills against each other to win talismans. Other festivals are still based on physical contests between men, such as the bouts held in the mud of paddyfields and in the soot of New Year fires to secure a good harvest, and the Nomaoi matsuri festival, in which mounted samurai compete for three sacred pennants. In summer, young people can be seen beating huge drums, carrying bamboo cannons and enormous scaffolds of lanterns, or pulling gigantic wagons. As for the Buddhists, they prefer to practise martial arts and walking on hot coals. Men are not the only ones to test their strength and powers of self-denial – women do it too, and sometimes in very strange ways. In 1900, during the restoration of the Higashi Hongan-ji temple in Kyoto, while the men contributed their physical work, the women donated their hair so that cables could be woven to lift the heavy beams of the building's framework.

▶▶Ritual entry into the ring, performed by a great sumo champion. The *sumotori* – wearing a brocade apron adorned with good luck symbols, and the coiled belt, symbol of Shinto – is accompanied by two wrestlers who act as page-boy and sword-carrier.

1. Louis Aubert,
Paix japonaise
[The Japanese Concept of Peace],
Paris, Colin, 1906.

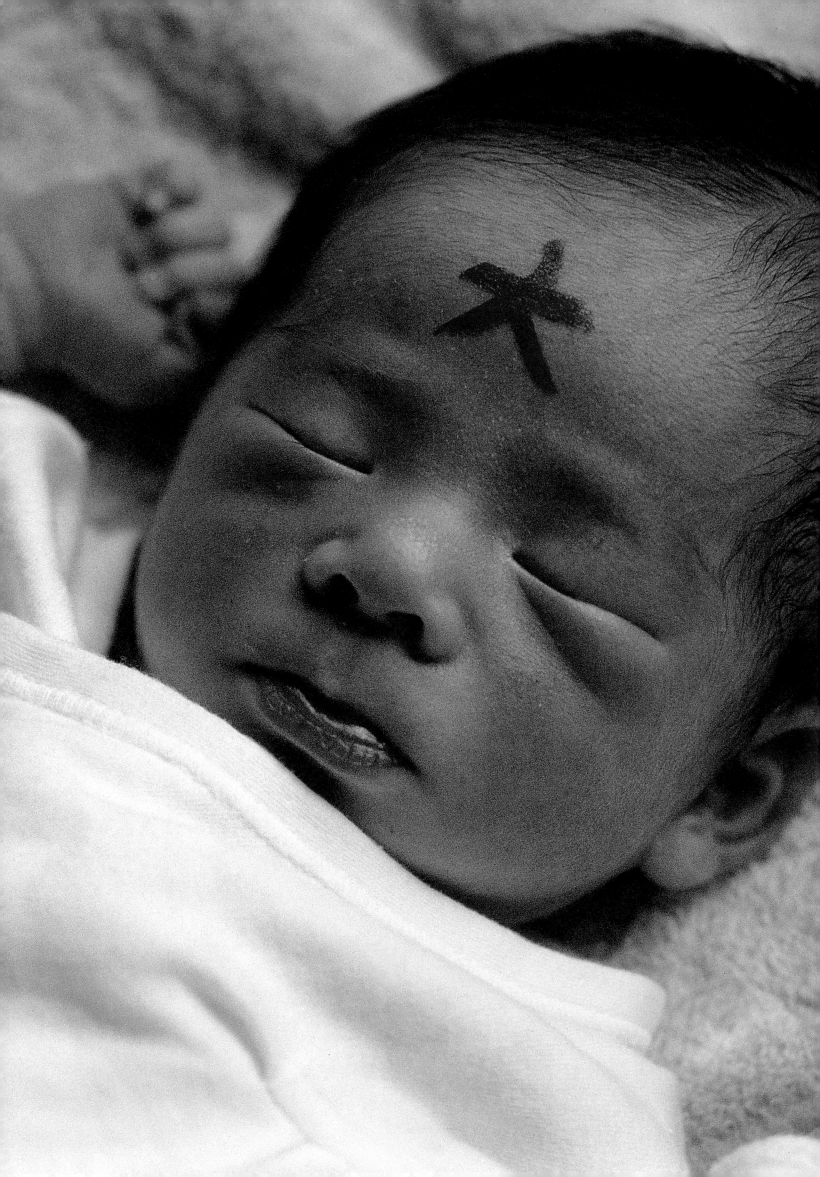

Born under the sign of the gods

From birth, children are placed under the sign of the divinities. At one time it was customary, on a child's seventh day of life, to mark the ideogram meaning 'great' on its forehead in red ink, to 'tease the spirits'. In some places, the ideogram meaning 'dog' was preferred, to protect the child from smallpox. For girls, the ideogram for 'small' was used, which immediately placed them in a subordinate position in society. At the same time, the child was given its first name and the heads of boys were shaved, leaving only a small lock on the nape of the neck. Even today, gifts of congratulation for the happy event are given during the first week, except for the fourth day, since the number four has the same sound as the ideogram for 'death'. A month after birth, the child is presented for the first time to the tutelary gods of its district. This visit to a shrine is an extremely important act, the child's opportunity to take part in its first Shinto purification sacrament. As a rule, the child is presented on the 30th day if it is a boy, and on the 32nd or 33rd day if it is a girl. Wearing an *ubu-gi*, a special kimono bearing the family coat of arms, the child is taken to the shrine, usually by the paternal grandmother, for the mother is still considered impure. There it is given a papier-mâché dog, which is supposed to protect it and help it to grow. The baby's first New Year is also a solemn event. That day is celebrated as its first birthday, and on the following 1 January, regardless of the month in which the child was born, it becomes two years old. Traditionally, a boy is given a gift of a bow and a girl a racket for playing ball. On the 120th day, when the child has one or two teeth, it is given its first meal, but it is rarely weaned before the age of two or three, or even four or five.

▲ Carried on its mother's back, the child takes part from birth in Japanese social life.

◀ A child in its mother's arms wears its first ceremonial kimono, the *ubu-gi*, for its presentation at the shrine.

◀ On a boy's first visit to the shrine, the ideogram *dai*, meaning great, is written on his forehead.

Bathing and harmony

From their earliest childhood, the Japanese are accustomed to bathing every day – an almost sacred purification rite without which they would not be worthy of being regarded as human. While the gods have dotted the archipelago with thousands of thermal springs, the Japanese have discovered holiness in the water of their own domestic baths, which are traditionally made of cedar wood. In Japan people do not bathe to wash, but to renew themselves and to enter into harmony with the fundamental rhythms of nature. Although bathing is much appreciated in winter, in summer it is essential to cope with the humid heat. At the end of the 19th century, when prudishness became one of the new virtues being adopted in Japan, mixed public baths were banned, though with little success. Since 1945, however, despite the Japanese saying 'nudity is seen but not looked at', the sexes have been kept completely separate in the *sento* (public baths), hot springs and open-air baths. In the 1930s, Tokyo had more than a thousand bathing establishments. During the 1960s, as houses became Westernised, bathrooms made the *sento* obsolete, but people continued to visit them for pleasure and to enjoy their relaxed atmosphere, especially older people, for whom they remained a rare treat. Hot water, at an average temperature of 42°C (108°F), allows the pores to dilate and the body to expel its toxins. Strangely, however, bathers are expected to leave the water as clean as they found it. At home, and at the *sento*, bathers soap and rinse themselves outside the bath before immersing themselves, perfectly clean, in water that will be used by the whole family. Morning baths are frowned upon as a habit of lazy people, who do not leave for work as soon as they have got up. On the other hand, an evening bath is absolutely necessary.

◀ Family bath in a hot spring at the Gero thermal spa in the Japanese Alps.

▶ 'Outdoor' baths in a cave on the Izu peninsula. The cave's vagina-like shape explains the presence of the phallic statue. Some baths are reserved for men, and others for women.

▼ Family bath in the 1920s. On the right, a female servant is stoking the fire that heats the water in the cypress-wood bathtub.

Water
and salt

Before the entrance to every Shinto shrine is a basin where the faithful can perform a token ablution before entering the sacred enclosure. This consists of washing the hands, beginning with the left, and rinsing the mouth, so as to arrive before the divinities pure in body and spirit. The origin of this rite supposedly goes back to when the god Izanagi, returning from the kingdom of the underworld, where he had gone to seek his dead spouse Izanami, plunged into the waters of a river to rid himself of the underworld's putrid fumes. This ritual can be performed directly in a river close to, or on the way to, a sacred place such as Mount Fuji. It is also possible to immerse oneself totally in the sea. Buddhists meditating under a waterfall are following the same principle, which serves symbolically to cleanse the spirit. A place, too, can be purified by throwing handfuls of salt over it, as sumo wrestlers do to sanctify the arena before each bout. In some places it is still customary to toss a pinch of salt into the fire to drive out demons before meat is cooked. Formerly, meat was seen as suspect and rarely eaten. After attending a funeral, it is forbidden to enter a house without first 'requesting the salt' and having it sprinkled over one's body by the mistress of the house. This method of driving away bad luck can sometimes be seen on the threshold of shops, in the form of three small pyramids of salt. Demons do not dare to cross this magic barrier, but if a customer entering a restaurant should accidentally knock into one of them, this would be seen as highly favourable. By the door of the temple of Asakusa Kannon in Tokyo, some of the followers of 'Jizo the salt taster' offer small dishes of salt to the divinity in order to be purified themselves.

◀ Kintaro, a child-hero in folk tales, practises a *misogi* purification rite under a waterfall, protected by two of his allies from the animal kingdom, a monkey and a rabbit. (Print by Yoshitoyo, mid-19th century.)

▶ Jizo the 'salt taster', in the Asakusa Kannon or Senso-ji temple, Tokyo.

▶▶ *Yamabushi* monks light the fire before a fire-walking rite. At their feet is the pile of salt used to purify the faithful before they make the crossing.

Fire
rituals

While adherents of Shinto mainly practise purification with salt and water, Buddhists prefer purification by fire, since the passions must be 'burned off'. This is why the rites of esoteric sects include the *goma* ritual, which consists of burning wooden blocks on which the faithful have written their 'confessions'. An identical, but more spectacular ritual is performed by the *yamabushi* monks when they walk on fire. They follow an ascetic way of life, known as *shugendo*, which owes as much to esoteric Buddhism as to Shinto and to religious Taoism, which promises immortality. Their main activity is the quest for their true inner nature, through various techniques designed to take them out of themselves, such as climbing mountains, walking to the limits of exhaustion, meditating under a waterfall, retreating to a cave and walking on fire. They also use magic, act as oracles and are thought to practise witchcraft. The ceremony, intended to guard against fires and protect crossroads from traffic accidents, begins with setting a huge number of branches on fire. These produce a broad carpet of embers 30 cm (12 in) deep and at least 5 m (16 ft) long, aligned with the cardinal points of the compass. After exorcising the place and invoking the god of water to come down from the moon and drive away the god of fire, the monks, dressed in white, walk across the live embers, led by the most senior. They are followed by volunteers of all ages, children, adults and the elderly, all of whom have just been purified in the Shinto manner. Immediately beforehand, each of them steps on a pile of salt placed at the beginning of the carpet of embers, and immediately after walking over the fire the faithful step on a second pile of salt placed next to the seat of the senior monk, who blesses them.

▲ A young girl crosses the carpet of embers during the fire-walking at the annual Hachioji festival.

▼ Two monks of the esoteric *tendai* sect carry out a *goma* ritual at the Senso-ji temple in Tokyo.

◄ A *yamabushi* monk putting cypress wood tablets on the fire, on which the faithful have written their lists of passions to be 'burned off'.

Sister-dolls
and paper dogs

Before the arrival of the Western practice of vaccination, the battle against illness was fought by a host of popular exorcisms. Many have fallen out of use, but traces of them can be found in some festivals, in certain toys and many folk remedies. The commonest way of driving out illness is to make substitute effigies from paper or sometimes straw, and rub the body so that they symbolically take off all the impurities. At New Year festivals these are burned or thrown into a river and a new set is made for the coming year. Friends may be given *ane-sama-ningyo*, faceless 'sister-dolls', to protect them from illness. At *nagashi-bina* festivals, celebrated on 3 March in the Tottori region, the custom is to let the dolls drift with the current in a small circular boat made of straw, each containing a pair of paper dolls, so as to drive away ill luck, enjoy good health and hope for a happy marriage. It is also possible to purify oneself by rubbing straw ash into parts of the body that are tired or affected by illness, or by rolling in the mud of recently worked paddy-fields. Another technique consists of rubbing or washing the parts of a statue that correspond to the areas of the body that are affected. The effigy of the physician Binzuru Sonja, one of Buddha's 13 disciples, is much sought after and can often be seen seated on a chair at the entrance to temples. The other main group of protective measures relies on prophylactic animals. A papier-mâché dog is one of the commonest. When placed behind the pillow of a woman about to give birth, it acts as a charm to ensure a trouble-free delivery. When it is given to a child at birth, it protects

▲ A prophylactic dog in papier-mâché, in the Shizuoka style, which is believed to ease childbirth and protect children from smallpox.

▼ Wooden tablets, known as *ema*, offered by geisha making wishes at the shrine in Kyoto's Gion district.

◄ Sheets of paper, called *senkaji fuda*, stuck to the beams of temples. These have been left by pilgrims or people who have vowed to visit a thousand temples to obtain a cure for a loved one.

it from smallpox, an illness which formerly was a great scourge, killing large numbers of children. For adults who contracted it, or who suffered from skin conditions, one way of exorcising their disease was to immerse themselves in the waters of a lake, wearing a broad hat, until it floated on the surface, taking the scales of skin with it.

Prevention being better than cure, it is enough to use objects that give symbolic protection. For example, if someone is prone to illnesses affecting their eyes, an offering can be made at a shrine of small wooden tablets inscribed with the syllabic sign *me*, meaning 'eye'. The geisha have developed their own protective system, particularly to cover their hairstyles and their combs. Since their high wooden clogs put them at risk of falling, they often wear an ornament in the shape of a colocynth, a plant that floats when dried and is supposed to make their bodies lighter. It is also possible simply to pray for a loved one to be cured. The *senkaji fuda*, the 'cards of the thousand temples', which visitors glue to the wooden framework of each temple they visit, are living proof of this belief. However, it can be enough to make only a hundred or so visits, or to make the 'hundred steps' around a religious building. According to tradition, the figure 1,000 is expressive of happiness and is associated with the idea of healing, as in the practice of making 'a thousand cranes' (birds) in origami to ensure someone's full recovery. There are many who still remember Sadako, a young girl suffering from radiation after the atom bomb was dropped on Hiroshima, who vowed to make a thousand origami of cranes before dying. To help her in her symbolic struggle against death, thousands of Japanese children folded the well-known outline of the *tsuru*, the bird which brings good luck in their country.

▶ Doll in the Shizuoka style of 'sister-doll'. These *ane-sama-ningyo* are faceless, so that they can represent anyone and take on that person's illnesses.

◀ Household gods protect the kitchen of a traditional house in Kyoto.

▼ *Nagashi-bina* from the Tottori region: a pair of dolls on a bed of rice straw, which is left to drift down a river to carry away bad luck and illness.

▶ Hiroshima memorial dedicated to Sasaki Sadako, the young girl who died from the effects of radiation.

◀ Offerings in the form of garlands with 'a thousand cranes' hang in a small religious building which combines the two religions of Shinto and Buddhism.

'Must I travel alone,
apart from everyone and weeping,
This road that leads to the land of death?'
Izumi Shikibu (974–1034)

Zen meditations

▲ Buddhas are always shown seated in the lotus position. What is unusual about these figures, dating from 985, is that the Buddha Amida's assistants are kneeling, in the Japanese manner. Ojo-koraku-in chapel, Sanzen-in Buddhist temple, Kyoto.

▶ Buddhist statue of Jizo *bosatsu*, the Ksitigarbha *bodhisattva*, protector of dead children and travellers. The figure wears the straw hat worn by pilgrims.

▼ A master performs the tea ceremony, one of the active forms of Zen meditation.

In Zen Buddhism, the body is inseparably linked to meditation. The latter is not just a therapeutic activity but a search for emptiness, because external reality can only be perceived in the form of illusion. As one Buddhist maxim states, 'The eye cannot see itself, the hand cannot seize itself and the mind cannot grasp itself.' Spiritual peace can be achieved only by immediate intuition, not by any rational process. While Shinto demands that its followers do what must be done when the moment comes, with no other obligation than that of satisfying the gods, Zen Buddhism disciplines the body in order to be able to escape from it more effectively. This is true of the remarkable arts of Zen, which are divided into passive and active meditation. The passive type, which is a purely non-mental activity, is practised seated in the posture known as *zazen*, in a room presided over by a statue of Monju bosatsu, the *bodhisattva* of the intellect, for truth can only be attained in the most profound internal silence. The meditator adopts the 'lotus' position and controls his or her breathing so as to be able to hear the breath moving along the spine and coming to rest at a point between the eyes. When the mind disconnects and the body becomes taut, the meditator asks for the *kyosaku*, a rod with which a monk strikes the fleshy area at the base of the neck, dense with acupuncture points, to bring the meditator back to a state of concentration. Contemplative meditation facing a sand garden is part of this 'constructive activity'. In active meditation, martial arts, arts of etiquette such as the tea ceremony, flower arranging, the arts of incense and callig-raphy, as well as gathering alms for monks, are all testing disciplines or rituals, which, by taking participants outside the self, allow enlightenment to be gradually attained.

▲ The superior of the Daisen-in temple in Kyoto meditates before the dry garden, representing the Sea of Tranquillity that leads to Paradise in the West.

▶ The lotus position of Zen meditation, which allows mental and physical energy to flow through the body without hindrance.

▶ A Zen monk appeals for money to buy food in a Kyoto street.

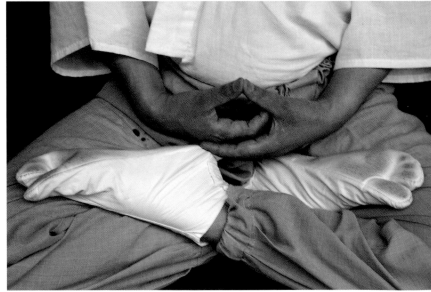

'If one can become a Buddha simply by sitting down and meditating, then a toad such as I, who have sat down ever since birth, would long ago have achieved Enlightenment and become a Buddha.'
Sengai, painter (1750–1837)

Servants
of the gods

In Shinto, white is the hue of the gods and red the hue of celebration. When officiating, the priest wears a white kimono and a *hakama*, a skirt-like pair of trousers, whose hue varies according to the priest's rank but which is usually pale blue. When making offerings, the priest puts a brocade robe in the style of ancient court dress over these garments. The *miko*, the young virgins who enter the shrine as servants of the *kami*, wear a white kimono and a red *hakama* when going about their daily tasks. At ceremonies and dances, they wear a white garment on top with wide, open sleeves and decorated with good-luck symbols such as pine trees and cranes; on their hair they also wear a diadem, either in gilt metal or made of fresh leaves of the *sakaki*, the sacred tree of Shinto. Their hair, which may be either real or artificial, falls down their back and is gathered together by red and white fasteners like those worn by princesses in the Heian period. When he is not wearing work clothes, a Buddhist monk wears, over his kimono, the item of clothing most vital to his role: the *kesa*, which recalls the shroud in which Buddha wrapped himself before setting out on his travels, convinced that asceticism was futile as a route to salvation. This piece of material, a Japanese version of the Indian gown, which is draped over the left shoulder and winds round the body to the right, has become the very symbol of Buddhism. It is made up of several pieces, always an odd number and arranged as a quincunx. A monk generally owns three of these. A special type of small *kesa*, made up of five pieces of material, is worn by Zen monks as part of their work clothing. It looks like a bag attached to the wearer's neck which hangs down over the stomach, but it does not now serve any practical purpose.

▲ The rice-planting ceremony in the enclosure of the Fushimi Inari shrine, near Kyoto. These young women are the *miko* of this shrine, which is dedicated to the god Inari, the *kami* of cereals.

▼ A carpenter's album, showing the Shinto gods Taoki and Hijo-sajiri, considered the *kami* of architecture for having built the first dancing platform or stage, which tempted the sun goddess to emerge from her retreat.

◀ Shinto priests and *miko*, in their white ceremonial garments, revere the spirits of the Tokugawa *shogun* at the Futara-san mausoleum in Nikko.

礼儀 The social body

'The Japanese do not admire people in themselves, but rather the virtues they symbolise,' stated Louis Frédéric. However, more often than not they are prisoners of the rites with which they surround themselves. As well as Buddhism and Shinto, both great purveyors of precepts, Japan has a third system of ideas, Confucianism, based on harmonious relations between people and designed to regulate the rights and obligations of all. Introduced to the country at the time of the earliest contacts with China, it originally formed the basis of the Imperial Court's etiquette before gradually becoming popular throughout Japanese society. Confucianism did not limit itself to setting the rules of etiquette, but established a practical code of ethics, illustrated by a series of edifying stories and simple precepts suitable for educating young Japanese. During the reign of the *shogun* Tokugawa, neo-Confucianism became part of the art of government, and society was ordered into a strict hierarchy of social classes: warriors, peasants, craftsmen and merchants. The pariah class was not mentioned. Although Confucianism was an agnostic philosophy, it encouraged the cult of ancestor worship and of keeping faith with the memory of the dead in the same way as Buddhism and Shinto – thus justifying its adoption by all people. Confucian 'classics' were published, containing the rules governing the life of each class, based on a series of duties of obedience to a superior authority: junior-senior, parents-child, master-pupil, husband-wife, lord-vassal, right up to the emperor himself, who was accountable to the sun goddess, his ancestor.

Great importance was attached to filial piety; one of the most popular books in Japan at the time was a collection of legends entitled *The Twenty-Four Models of Filial Piety*. It taught that filial piety lay at the foundation of all forms of authority, especially that of a master, who was regarded as the 'father of the mind'. Over the centuries this model became so strong that it culminated in the establishment of a system in which loyalty, pushed to its extreme, could be taken as far as sacrificing one's life when parents, a lord or a teacher were dishonoured. As *The Education of Young People*, dating from the 9th century, declares: 'Your father and mother are like heaven and earth: your tutor and your master are like the sun and the moon. Your other relatives are like reeds. Your wife is nothing but a useless stone.' From the outset, women were the chosen target of Confucian censors. According to an old custom, female babies were to be left on the floorboards for three days after their birth, to emphasise the difference

Marriage is a very important social act in Japanese society. The future bride, seen here wearing a wig in the style of the Edo period, is made up in an old-fashioned manner so that the white face paint prevents her betraying emotion.

39

between men's 'celestial' nature and the 'terrestrial' nature of women. This particular practice was derived from the rules set out at the beginning of the 18th century by Kaibara Ekiken in his *Great Education for Women*, a book designed to manage all aspects of women's behaviour – chiefly their duties. The author especially stressed the need to control women's sensuality, not for puritanical reasons but because the passion of love could lead to scandal, and thus risked the breakdown of law and order.

At the end of the 19th century, with the fall of military government and the restoration of the Meiji emperor, Japan became a member of the international community and the doctrine of the *shogun* no longer regulated society. The first result of the introduction of Western civilisation was a reduction in the influence of ceremony and ritual, which only survived in arts practised for pleasure such as *ikebana*, the tea ceremony and certain martial arts. In everyday life, however, the rules changed little and they are still widely applied today. They govern how people greet each other, present gifts, visit temples, bathe, eat and sleep in the Japanese manner, style their hair and dress according to circumstances, attend funerals, take part in festivals, and how women and men behave towards each other in public. The tradition of arranged marriages is still widely followed; this demands the services of an influential and wise person, a *nakodo*, whose job it is to act as an intermediary between the two families, look after the social aspects of the union, ensure that correct practice is followed and, for the rest of his or her life, to act as a godparent to the couple. Based on respect and reason, the arranged marriage is preferred to one based on passionate love, which does not allow the forging of bonds strong enough to ensure the family's prosperity and honour the names of their ancestors. Formerly, divorces were rare: it was as shameful for a woman to marry twice as it was for a samurai to serve two masters.

Japanese life still involves certain obligations, which, although not derived from Confucianism, sometimes contain echoes of it. A Japanese person takes on, from birth and for life, a set of duties that must be fulfilled, to the emperor, to parents, to a superior, and especially to a master. Each person has *gimu* and *giri* – a series of unavoidable and unchanging debts. *Gimu* involves several duties, which are generally accepted, the chief ones being unflinching devotion to the emperor, the state, parents and ancestors. *Giri* are a series of moral obligations that are 'fulfilled against one's will so as not to owe the world an apology'.[2] There are two *giri*: one owed to the outside world, the other to oneself. The first more often than not involves returning a favour received: an invitation or a present. The second demands that a person keep their name untainted by any censure, and cleanse their honour following any insult or accusation. A married woman must fulfil both sets of obligations: *gimu* to her parents and *giri* to her in-laws, which, in the event of conflict between the two, produces an insoluble dilemma. These principles often lead to a sort of indifference to other people when in a crowd – the only place where the system of obligations does not apply, and whose expressionless members are often referred to as 'faces about which nothing is known'. Oddly, in a country where frugality and modesty are virtues, the only havens, the only places where people can burst out of the straitjacket of their obligations, are the public baths or the bar where people go to get drunk with their colleagues. In the former, nudity shatters convention, while in the latter the loosening of inhibitions due to too much alcohol frees the individual from his responsibilities and allows him to speak his mind openly, which is forbidden at work.

The principles and norms of social behaviour are therefore all dictated by external appearances, but what is most important is what remains hidden and unsaid: the true intention. Greetings, smiles, modesty and propriety avoid burdening someone else with something they may not be able to tolerate. Uniforms and dress codes are not designed to make people appear banal, as in the West. On the contrary, they assert one's belonging to a group, to a community that lives and thinks in a certain way. When young people in search of their individual destiny criticise society's conformity by dressing up in eccentric clothes and wearing strange make-up and hairstyles, they are merely conforming unconsciously to their elders' principles. The great majority of primary school children wear uniforms. Those of the very youngest – round straw or felt hats, and bright jackets – have an engaging 'retro' quality, but those of male secondary school pupils, inspired by 19th-century Germany, are more severe, with buttoned 'Russian-style' collars, drainpipe trousers and flat caps. Those of female secondary pupils feed Japanese men's fantasies with their sailor-style collars, knee-length pleated skirts and white socks. Family men are hardly any more avant-garde: today's 'salaryman' proclaims his rank and responsibilities through his unvaryingly dark suit, white shirt and discreet tie. When he is relaxing, his sports, golf, fishing or baseball outfit is always as close as possible to those worn by successful professionals and champions. Women's kimonos, too, are a uniform, regulated by many precise rules: length of sleeve, shape of knot, the way they match the seasons, and the way the decorative motifs run along the seams of the sleeves. As for artists, they apparently cannot live without a beret and long, unkempt hair.

2. Ruth Benedict,
Le Chrysanthème et le sabre
[The Chrysanthemum and the Sword],
Éditions Picquier, Paris, 1987.

'From an early age,
the Western child learns to protect himself
and acquire a degree of immunity from the
bacterium known as *other people*.

The Japanese, however, know nothing
of that immunity.'

Keiko Yamanaka, *The remote archipelago*.

Smiles
and greetings

One feature of Japan is the extreme politeness its inhabitants display at all times. From birth, a Japanese child is taught to bow. As it is carried on its mother's back, the child bends forward with her at every encounter. The bow is a rather complex act, which depends on the relationship between the two people concerned, their relative social status and their sex. A bow can be made either seated or standing and, in either case, there are three degrees of inclination of the head and body. The most respectful is the *saikeirei*: this is made in a place of prayer, before the national flag or before a very important person. The person bowing looks at the person being bowed to, and gradually leans forward until their body and head are at 45 degrees, while the hands, with fingers straight, slide down to the knees (for a woman) or are pressed to the sides of the body (for a man). This position must be maintained for three seconds. The two other bows are less elaborate: the angle of inclination is smaller and the position is held for a shorter time. Bowing in a room with *tatami* (mats) means that one is sitting down: then the hands are placed in front of the knees with the fingers touching, and the body is bent double until the head brushes them. In the least formal bow, women are allowed to touch the floor only with their fingers, and men can keep their hands on their knees.

Bowing to Shinto gods always begins with purification at a wash basin. The worshipper first bows before the shrine, then throws some money into the collecting box, and bows again, before raising the hands up to the shoulders and clapping twice to call the divinity. Finally, after praying and moving back a few paces, the worshipper bows for the last time. The Buddhist bow is called *gassho* ('hands together'). It need not start with a purification, apart from the smoke from the incense burner which is in front of all temples, but

▶ Worshippers bow before a Shinto shrine. To call the divinity, one of the young women is moving a thickly plaited rope to ring a bell, while the other claps her hands two or three times. The woman on the left is wearing the 'drum' knot, indicating that she is married.

▼ The deepest bow, the *saikeirei*, made here in a kneeling position to give thanks for a gift. The person on the right, who is receiving the present, must bow lower.

it must involve the giving of alms. With the hands placed together, the worshipper winds the rosary round all the fingers, but not the thumbs, so as to rub the beads together while praying. After a slight bow, the worshipper may go to ring the heavy bell outside the shrine, or burn some incense. In Japan, the first act of courtesy is a smile – not a happy, innocent smile, but the enigmatic one that Westerners find impenetrable. This apparently empty smile is in fact an essential convention for communicating shades of meaning. It acts as a double screen, designed both to control a person's inner emotions (thus sparing other people from them) and to protect that person from the emotions of others. It is polite for a subordinate to respond to a reproach by smiling and, if the criticism is repeated, to intensify the smile. This irrational response simply indicates that the person under-stands the situation and accepts that the criticism is justified. In this instance a smile is a means of avoiding shame, for 'Japan is more the land of shame than the land of guilt'. Since the individual's only sphere of morality is society, he or she is duty bound to preserve its harmony by never provoking direct confrontation or risking committing an inexcusable offence that would force others to pass judgement. Sometimes this principle of shame is pushed to extremes: it is not acceptable to help someone who has fallen to the ground, as this would oblige them to repay a debt that they might be unable to take on. Smiling is at once a truly disciplined aspect of behaviour, which reveals what remains unsaid, and it can also be a highly elegant gesture when it is a spontaneous expression, modestly hidden at once by a hand or a fan.

◄ The correct position for the hands on the thighs when seated wearing a kimono. This summer kimono, decorated with a wave motif, belongs to a young married woman, as can be seen from the way the *obiage*, the scarf that keeps the belt's cushion in place, slightly overlaps the top of the *obi*.

▼ A bow of the second category between two women friends. Since neither is socially superior to the other, their angles of inclination are identical. Each wears a young woman's spring kimono, with long sleeves and a protruding *obiage*.

►► In Japan, good breeding demands that laughter and smiles be hidden. Children are accustomed from an early age to conceal the discomfort caused by the sudden expression of a person's character. to do so, they raise their hands in front of their mouths, like these little girls in demon costumes, caught backstage at a theatre.

Young women today

Innocence, courtesy, submissiveness and virginity remain the traditional qualities of a young woman eligible for marriage. Although virginity is no longer seen as absolutely essential today, social 'purity' and the rejection of undesirable relationships are still strict requirements. Today, a young Japanese woman will work for a few years before marrying. As a result, there are large numbers of well-educated young women in the world of work: manual workers in electronics factories, hostesses, 'shrimp-women' tirelessly bowing to every customer in a department store while wiping the escalator rail with a white-gloved hand, and above all the unavoidable 'office flowers' responsible 'for tea rather than for filing'. They used to be known as 'BGs' (business girls) and later, slightly more respectfully, as 'OLs' – office ladies. Today the more active of them are often referred to, somewhat apprehensively, as 'career women'. It is these young women, constantly replaced by new blood, who give daily life in Japan its all-pervading atmosphere of youth and sweetness. While performing her duties – the pleasant welcome, attentive service, standard smile and sugary voice – a Japanese woman must suppress her own intelligence, adapt her appearance and moderate the sound of her voice to conform to a fantasy of the ideal young woman before she becomes a 'respectable woman'. By the age of 26 it is time for her to marry, if she is to avoid society's disapproval. Going beyond this age without being married invites suspicion; the victim tends to be labelled an 'old maid', which implies she is irredeemably bad-tempered and hysterical.

▲ Young 'shrimp women' in a department store.

◀ Japanese school uniforms are based on those of late 19th-century Germany. At the start of the school year secondary pupils are assembled and given their instructions for the coming year.

▼ Uniforms are worn from nursery school onwards, to allow the child to join a system based on belonging to a group and a social environment. Each school, whether state or private, has its own uniform.

'They have a feeling
for the poetry of things,
for nature's great, nebulous soul,
for the enchantment of flowers
and forests,
for silence and moonbeams ...'
Pierre Loti, *Mukashi, mukashi.*

▶ A young woman purifies
herself at a fountain in a tea
garden.

▲ ▶ A well brought-up young
girl must be familiar with
traditional skills, such as the tea
ceremony and flower arranging.
She should also play an
instrument such as the *koto*,
harp or piano.

The horns
of jealousy

Autumn is the wedding season in Japan, but weddings may not take place in November, the 'month without gods'. During the short ceremony the bride sits on her future husband's left. The priest begins by purifying the couple and congregation, then pours *sake* into the three nuptial cups which the couple must drink in three draughts to perform the *sansankudo* ('three times three is nine'), which seals the marriage. The newlyweds then bow before the altar to offer twigs of *sakaki* (a Japanese shrub) to the *kami*, and invite their two families to the wedding banquet, where auspicious dishes such as sea bream, a symbol of happiness, are served. Traditionally a Japanese woman will wear two or three kimonos in the course of her wedding day. The first, worn for the religious ceremony, is of white brocade – the hue of mourning – to indicate that she is dead for her own family and from now on belongs to her in-laws. For this reason her face must betray no sign of emotion and, to achieve this, must be heavily made up with white powder, the only remaining sign of seduction being her red-painted mouth and the exposed nape of her neck. She wears a wig in the Edo style, set with combs, hairpins and plumes on which she has placed a broad band of white silk that, traditionally, prevents the horns of jealousy from appearing. Later she will put on a less luxurious and more brightly hued kimono, or a Western wedding dress. If she comes from a traditional environment, custom demands that – after relinquishing her young girl's kimonos with their long sleeves and belt knotted in the shape of a sparrow or a butterfly – she adopts a more discreet kimono secured by a simple 'drum' knot, hides her nape under a close-fitting collar, and cuts her hair and styles it more severely. From now on, she is 'the one who lives in the background'.

▲ A couple bow to the divinities during a religious wedding ceremony, before exchanging consecrated cups of *sake*. The bride wears an Edo-style 'horn screen' over her hair.

▶ A 'horn screen' in the ancient style of Kyoto.

▶ The betrothed couple arrive at the shrine accompanied by the *nakodo*, a person who acts as intermediary between the two families and the future spouses. The bridegroom wears a *hakama* and a kimono decorated with his family's coat of arms, and the bride a special wedding kimono.

A respectable
woman

From feudal times until quite recently, any discussion of what defined a man involved a physical description of a person and an account of their manly behaviour. On the other hand, no reference to physical shape would be used to describe a 'respectable woman'. The essential quality of a Japanese woman was gauged by her gestures – her ability to convey a malleable character, reserve and willingness to serve – and to her voice, which, ideally, should be soft and measured. Through these she gave tangible proof of the power and sophistication of her husband. In society's eyes she was a wife and mother before being lovable or loved. The discreetness of her kimono, the shape of the knot in her belt, and the way she cut her hair were constant reminders of her status and duties. A respectable woman's life was governed by 'three submissions' – to her father, to her husband and to her eldest son. She was not to express openly the 'four emotions' of happiness, anger, sadness and joy. As a wife she was obliged for ever more to trot along three paces behind her husband, to pay in restaurants, carry luggage, and get up in the middle of the night to welcome him home. With the modernisation of Japan at the start of the 20th century, and especially as a result of American influence after the Second World War, manners gradually grew closer to those of the West, but in Japan, a country where the tiniest aspects of life were ritualised, the old customs died hard. They were, and still are, kept alive by the Japanese language itself: once she is married, a woman is no longer referred to by her first name, as she was as a young girl, or by her family name, like her husband, but in terms of 'the one who lives in the background', 'the inside of the house', or even as 'stupid woman'. She in turn should always use the title 'master' for her husband, whom she should 'look up to as to a divinity'.

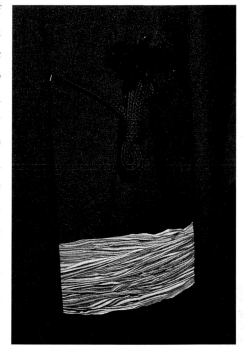

◀▲ Most Japanese clothes indicate a difference between men and women. The *haori*, for example, is a half-length jacket worn over a kimono, fastened at the front with a decorative knot. A woman's knot hangs downwards, a man's points upwards. The man's belt is also narrower than the woman's *obi*.

The right to be different

▲ Young people known as 'young bamboo shoots', dressed in retro US 1960s style, dance in Tokyo's Yoyogi Park.

▶ A modern young couple, with dyed hair and a free and easy manner. Until very recently such a manner of behaving was regarded as unacceptable.

According to the proverb, the nail that sticks out invites the hammer. Nevertheless, dreaming is allowed, and young Japanese women who achieve independence and earn their living in the unorthodox areas of Japanese life, such as the fashionable worlds of art, fashion and pop music, are reluctant to be drafted into the parade of 'young girls in a box' destined for marriage. More independent, and therefore misunderstood, they are ideal objects for the fantasies of Japanese men – the very men who dread and condemn their independence. But defiance of convention can also be acceptable if it takes the form of youthful exuberance, especially if this is contained. The *takenoko* ('young bamboo shoots'), aged 15 or 16, who gather every weekend in the avenues of Tokyo's Yoyogi Park, are thus asserting their right to be different, dancing themselves to exhaustion in glittering lamé outfits, black leather blousons, polka-dot miniskirts and fluorescent shirts. These boys and girls believe they are experiencing individual freedom for the first time, yet they know full well that they will soon step back into line. But there are also Japanese adolescents who no longer respect custom and who are no longer understood. While no-one is shocked today by young people holding hands in the street, and hair dyed orange is a tolerated craze, the aggressive drug addicts sprawled at station exits and the increasing violence of young people are intimidating proof that 'harmony' no longer rules in Japanese life to the extent it once did. As an indignant Paul Claudel wrote at the beginning of the 20th century: 'The dirty and scruffy appearance of these young people in European clothing, contrasting with the dignity, elegance and cleanliness of the native dress, was one of the saddest sights in Tokyo.'

◀ In Tokyo's Yoyogi Park, fans of US rock 'n' roll nostalgia always form a separate group with their motorbikes. With black blousons and gelled hair, some shave part of their scalp to accentuate the outline of their hairstyle.

▶ A mendicant plays a long bamboo flute, his face hidden by a pleated hat like the itinerant monks of former times.

'The river's flow is endless,
The same water never returns,
The bubbles in the lake burst, new ones form
None endures.
Such is man, his works, his time on earth.'
    Kamo no Chomei (1156–1216) *Hojoki*.
    Monk and poet.

芸者

The body
in love

Unlike the Judaeo-Christian West, which insists on seeing sex as inseparable from evil, Japan does not condemn pleasure in itself. Pleasure does not imply any personal guilt. The only condition placed upon it is, according to Confucian morality, that it should not threaten law and order or tarnish someone's name with an indelible stain. Japanese sexuality therefore has more to do with immediate gratification than with the Western concept of love.

For many centuries prostitution was even considered an art. On 31 March 1958, Tokyo's Yoshiwara district closed its doors for the last time. Two years earlier, Mizoguchi had filmed *Street of Shame* in this famous Edo-period red-light district, which had existed since 1617. Prostitutes have carried on their profession since the earliest times, and from the 10th century onwards dancers sometimes offered their body in exchange for presents. Organised prostitution was established in the 12th century and, a hundred years later, the profession was recognised, controlled, and taxed by the authorities. Under the reign of the *shogun* during the Edo period, prostitution was permanently confined to special districts surrounded by moats and high walls, such as Shimabara in Kyoto, Shinmachi in Osaka, and Yoshiwara in Edo. In poor districts, girls were sold to 'tea houses' to feed their families, or to allow the family's son to continue to honour its ancestors. Some of these attained the rank of geisha, but most became common prostitutes, displayed in the front windows of 'green houses' to attract passers-by. Courtesans – geisha – were classified according to their beauty, their excellence in practising the arts, and even the quality of their genitalia. Although at the beginning of the 20th century there were 30,000 geisha practising their arts, today only a few thousand are left, seducing only through their artistic talents in a few places such as the Gion district of Kyoto.

The industry known as *ura* ('what is hidden'), which has been thriving since the 1980s, is now run by the *yakuza* in 'Turkish baths', 'pink salons', 'knickerless cafés' and other places of fantasy in Japan's big cities. These offer a brief illusion, a 'subsidised' relationship, novel forms of voyeurism, hostesses in bars that provide a willing ear, and the dream of a sex tour in Thailand, Korea or the Philippines.

In Buddhism, sex is an integral part of human nature; in Shinto, it is even the chief element in many celebrations. Nevertheless, there are limits to the expression of sexuality in a society dominated, to a greater or lesser extent, by Confucian ethics.

Paradoxically, eroticism in Japan hinges on the idea of veiled beauty, even though there is no moral constraint on the expression of sexuality.

This 'morality' is not linked to the idea of personal guilt but to social shame in the event of an individual's sexual exploits threatening his good name. Sexuality is therefore expressed in more discreet, refined ways; fetishism of the body still depends largely on what is being concealed. While the Japanese body shrinks from exposing its nakedness, what counts is what is hinted at or sparingly revealed by clothes. The sensuality of the kimono is thus one of Japan's great traditional arts. A woman's intimate body, revealed in the warmth of its folds as in the secrecy of a futon, is reduced to the adoration of the grain of her skin, the nape of her neck or her foot. Hair, above all, has always been a mark of a woman's beauty, and in certain folk myths it was even thought that her soul resided there. As for male erotic appeal, men do not really aspire to it; their social status and authority are their only weapons of seduction. However, traditionally a man in a kimono knows, as a woman does, how to send almost imperceptible signals by the way the collar is left open, a belt is lowered and, sometimes, through certain stylised gestures.

In contrast to the erotic subtleties of the kimono, nudity, which is normally avoided through modesty, is flaunted when it becomes a symbol of fertility or primitive purity during rites connected to the land. Shrines are dedicated to the phallus and display it in full anatomical detail, as in those so-called Japanese prints formerly used for sex education. The body is also openly displayed, apparently quite acceptably, to everyone from innocent children to experienced adults in the cheap graphic stories that are read by everyone when they are packed into a train or underground carriage. These erotic *manga* are for the most part extremely violent, and depict the various sexual techniques in a clinical manner. However, unlike the prints of the past, the *manga* present an endless catalogue of every conceivable sexual perversion and cruelty. The same is true of girls' magazines, which are often more shocking than those aimed at men or boys. Strangely, however, in such a permissive society, the law forbids the depiction of sexual organs or pubic hair, which drives the cartoonists to dream up a whole gallery of explicit graphic metaphors for penetration, ejaculation or the female sex organs. Classics of the genre include a train entering a tunnel, a catfish with bristling barbels, explosions, geysers and moist shellfish. Apart from these graphic fantasies, there are no specifically Japanese sexual specialities apart from a predilection for sado-masochism. Here it is usually women who dominate men, though popular and artistic imagery concentrates on images of women in bondage suffering the most brutal humiliation.

The attraction for young girls or Lolitas, known as *lolikon*, is perhaps the most notice-able Japanese fantasy. With the growth of video and the Internet, it makes more converts every day, people who literally fetishise images of students in provocative poses, even secondary-school girls on the threshold of puberty. However, Japanese men are reputedly more voyeuristic than active and, to indulge this 'culture', many young students have no qualms about working as hostesses in bars to fund their studies. In fact, they have taken the place of the traditional *maiko*, chattering and listening to the solitary outpourings of their clients – and going further if it suits them. Since virginity is no longer a requirement for marriage in Japan, these 'Lolitas' are becoming progressively younger and more experienced. They are no longer content to titillate by wearing a *sailor fuku* (the secondary school uniform), or by selling their used knickers, but pose for risqué pictures and take to casual prostitution to earn pocket money. The taste for their smooth-cheeked, cute and innocent look is shared not only by paedophile deviants but by young girls themselves, even the most shameless, who refuse to venture out of the reassuring world of child-hood. At work, as in the street, it is quite normal for girls to murmur with a voice like crystal, and to wear trinkets and scraps of fur attached to their handbags until the eve of their marriage.

Traditionally, being married is not about love but about family. Sexual love is practised only very rarely in the home, and much more in special places known as love hotels. Generally recognisable a long way off by their fake medieval architecture, these establishments for legitimate couples offer not only complete anonymity to clients but also a great variety of décor and surroundings: Hollywood-style bedrooms, beds shaped like cars or boats, walls covered with mirrors, and karaoke and video equipment. When satisfying their fantasies, modern Japanese men are reputedly not very romantic. They no longer want to know about swooning with love at the sight of a sleeve wet with tears, or to court a geisha for days on end for the privilege of hearing her play the *shamisen* while untying her sumptuous kimono. Japanese women, for their part, no longer want to wear the silk straitjacket that hampers their freedom. The Japanese male today wants his sex direct, without any associated emotions, and in this aesthetic of violence and submission the woman must always wear an expression of acute internal torment. Her curled toes and upturned eyes must also suggest her acceptance of the pleasure offered by the dominating male. In this eroticism of destruction and suffering, love – more than ever – is a fleeting, illusory and doomed beauty.

Love and kimonos

Although the word *ki-mono* means 'thing to be worn', conceptually it has more to do with the realm of emptiness, since the body it contains has no existence of its own. This emptiness that exists between the skin and the material is felt over the entire body, and was what gave the kimono its sensual elegance that astonished the first Western visitors to Japan. But the kimono is also a 'priestly' symbol, and it takes a certain ascetic discipline to wear it, renouncing the natural tendency to exaggerate gestures in favour of grace and restraint. Only a woman who likes it can wear it well and enjoy forgetting her own body inside it. The ideal of beauty for a Japanese woman depends above all on her smoothly curving shoulders, a waist that is not pronounced, and unobtrusive breasts. Consequently, the kimono tempts the eyes with very few elements of the body that are considered particularly sensual in Japan: small areas of skin without make-up, a glimpse of ankle, a languid hand, a masked smile. A kimono's collar is one of the most important pieces of jewellery a Japanese woman possesses, for it reveals or hides the nape of the neck, the high point of Japanese seduction. A well-bred woman must adjust it with reserve, whereas a courtesan deliberately pushes it back to invite admirers to explore the imagined warmth lower down, below the collar. Unlike the nape of the neck, the foot is one of the most erotic parts of the body in Japan. Since the kimono restricts the legs, Japanese women's feet are turned slightly inwards, which inevitably makes them walk on the front part of their feet. This sliding gait, devoid of aggression, gives a woman an eternal, light fragility which is highly seductive, and places emphasis on the feet, whose movements are accentuated by the immaculate white of the *tabi* (two-toed socks). And when a woman climbs a step, the glimpse of the skin of her leg, heightened by the delicate tone of the barely seen inner kimono, has a secret erotic power that invites the admirer to look further up her leg towards greater voluptuousness. A kimono has no buttons, and its belt is a weak barrier against any improper intrusion – at most, it can delay matters. A silk fortress on the point of falling, the *obi* was, naturally, refined by courtesans and actors, since 'green houses' and

▲ According to custom, a woman in a kimono must wear her hair raised in a chignon, to highlight her nape and allow her collar to lean slightly backwards.

◀ A young woman putting on the under-kimono, known as a *juban*. It is worn over a short chemise which goes next to the skin and has pockets which can be stuffed to fill out the hollows in the shoulders, hips and small of the back so that the kimono hangs better.

kabuki halls were places where eroticism could be freely expressed and where the kimono ruled supreme. The *obi* was knotted at the front, allowing its ends to hang to the ground – an invitation to untie them. This knot, like a spider with long brocade legs, was an open invitation to lovemaking and simultaneously represented embracing arms and the union of the sexes. The kimono also played an important part in the delicate play of sleeves, made a gesture more eloquent, or hindered it. The wrist, half revealed, was another seductive element. Formerly, the female body was a fetish only if it was hidden or revealed by movement. At the Heian court, where the long sleeves of the kimono were essential to convey the emotions of princesses and their suitors, these sleeves had become so long over the centuries that they touched the ground, further amplifying the expression of their feelings. Today, such play of sleeves remains a constant reminder of propriety, and an essential part of all arts, such as the tea ceremony or flower arranging. When a person is wearing a kimono, the arms and sleeves are always associated with the angle of inclination of the head, and thus with the internalisation of feelings; in everyday life, coquettishness likes to hide a smile, or embarrassment, behind a sleeve or a fan. This is why it has been said of the kimono that it is not so much a garment as a way of behaving.

▲ The actress Miyazono Junko in a prostitute's costume from the Edo period. The collar of her kimono, pushed far back, and her slightly undone hair indicate her status as a woman of easy virtue.

◄ A young girl refreshes herself from a stream. The shape of her kimono, the length of its sleeves and the width of her belt limit her movements, but for the Japanese these constraints are a manifestation of elegance and sensuality.

► In the Heian period, the ideal of beauty was a body reduced to a series of superimposed kimonos and a cascade of hair. Women at court wore a number of kimonos commensurate with their rank: the Empress wore 12.

►► A young woman uses a mirror to choose an *obi* and accessories to go with the design on her kimono.

Hairstyles

Since 'a woman's beauty is measured by the length of her hair', at one time hair was often considered more important than any other accessory in her dress. Magical properties were even attributed to it. Merely having untidy hair amounted to an admittance of total negligence, and a woman would spend the night before a romantic assignation combing her immensely long locks. At the Heian court a woman's figure was reduced to a long twirl of hair, black as 'crow's feathers' and 'cold and damp' to the touch, snaking through the folds of superimposed kimonos. During the Edo period, a great variety of styles of chignon proliferated in the cities. The most exuberant required a whole armoury of hair-slides, pins, combs and ribbons, not forgetting the camellia oil used to give the hair a brilliant shine. Hairstyles took a long time to arrange, and so they were only redone every five or six days, the wearer sleeping on a high pillow of lacquer ware or bamboo so as not to disturb its convolutions. The hair, which should be neither too thick nor too sparse, ideally formed a V-shaped point in the middle of the forehead known as a *karigane* (wild goose). This defined the edge of an area to be covered in make-up that was shaped like a mountain and symbolised Mount Fuji. Formerly, Japanese women whose hair was going white used to dye it so as not to inflict on others the sad fact of their ageing. Sometimes elderly women would even shave their heads completely, and renounce their worldly life. Even today, hairstyles are an essential element of feminine beauty, and no young woman can imagine getting married without a wig drawn up in the complicated Edo-period style of *shimada* chignons – even if it is then concealed under a white hood which is supposed to hide the horns of jealousy.

◀ Sharaku, *The Actor Sawamura Sojuro III in the Role of Ogishi Kurando*, about 1794. Musée Guimet, Paris.

▼ A collection of functional and decorative combs in box and camellia wood. Wives of samurai did not wear combs made of camellia wood: this flower, which fades abruptly while still in full bloom, was a bad omen for warriors.

▶ *Maiko* and geisha take great care of their hair. The chignon of a *maiko* takes its form from the style of the Edo period, and is much less elaborate than that of a geisha.

Sensualists

The word geisha appeared during the Edo period at the end of the 17th century when, in the closed district of Yoshiwara, new dances were developed that were freer and more expressive than those performed in noblemen's houses for the entertainment of warriors. These 'highly gifted dancers' were known from then on as geisha – 'those who excel in the arts' of the 'floating world' portrayed by artists in prints. This sensual world, which was as materialistic as it was hedonistic, was a product of the middle classes of Kyoto, Edo and Osaka, who frequented the 'avenues of flowers and willows' and indulged in the nocturnal pleasures of the 'green houses'. There, the wealthiest of these 'sensualists' entertained high-ranking courtesans – *tayu* or *oiran* – as an unquestionable mark of their power. These women, almost all of noble birth, were skilled in all the arts, took a pride in their appearance, respected propriety and made shrewd use of their intelligence and beauty. As young apprentices, called *maiko* in Kyoto, they had undergone a long period of training in elocution, singing, music, dancing and the arts of flower arranging, tea and incense, before taking the qualifying exam and going through *mizu-age*, the deflowering ceremony. Once they acquired the title of geisha, they were paid wages according to the number of incense sticks burned during their work, when they were also accompanied by more than one *maiko*. The geisha thus raised seduction to the level of a set of aesthetic principles in which the sophisticated science of preliminaries was constantly redefined, obliging their admirers to respect all the rules of their profession.

▲ Utamaro, *Portrait of the Celebrated Oiran Hanaogi*, about 1794, N. Lagane Collection, Paris. The *obi* worn by courtesans was knotted at the front, and was sometimes so bulky that it was called *manaita* – 'board to be cut up'.

▼ A *kabuki manaita*. The water and iris motifs denote prostitution.

◀ A *maiko* daydreams at the window of a Western fashion boutique.

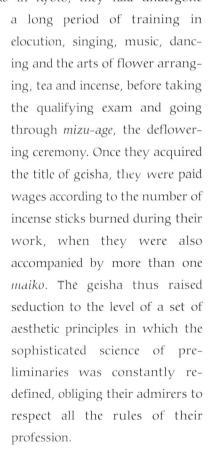

'For him, this woman's foot represented a
sort of jewel of youthful flesh. The arrangement of the
five delicate toes, from the big to the little toe,
the shade of the nails which cedes nothing to the pale pink
shells that can be gathered on the beach of Enoshima,
the roundness of the heel, like the oval of a pebble, the freshness
of the skin which seemed perpetually caressed
by pure water flowing between rocks: that was the very
foot that would feed on the blood of a man and trample
upon his dead body.'
Tanizaki Junichiro, *Tattoo*,
(translated by Madeleine Lévy)

▲ A *maiko* opens a paper screen. Her *obi*, unlike that of a young girl, is not knotted in the shape of a bird or a butterfly; instead, its ends are left hanging loose.

▼ Flat fan of a *maiko*. It bears the girl's name – Tsunemaru – and that of the geisha house to which she belongs.

▶ The Japanese skin has often been praised by poets for its delicacy and transparency, but in the make-up of a *maiko* its grain is only revealed by the white of the powder applied to it.

Artists
in seduction

The geisha is a time-honoured icon of seduction in Japan, and remains the ideal of seduction today. This aesthete of love is now free in body and heart, because the abolition of prostitution in 1958 clearly separated bar hostesses and prostitutes from the real geisha. According to Japanese law, the apprenticeship for this profession begins at the age of 16. Under the strict discipline of a godmother-geisha, the young apprentice is initiated, as in the past, in the skills of entertainment and deportment. Later, she will perfect her skills in making herself up and perfecting her clothing down to the last detail, conducting conversation and dealing in worldly eroticism. Then she will be able to accompany her seniors to their evening engagements. As in the Edo period, the geisha enhances her seductive powers by shaving her eyebrows and redrawing them with a black pencil, and she continues to wear the complex *shimada* chignon which stops her hair falling on to her nape. She owns, on average, about 15 sumptuous kimonos. These have stronger hues and bolder, broader decorative motifs than those of a *maiko*. A *maiko* is distinguishable from her seniors by her less voluminous but more decorative hairstyle, the fresher hues and motifs of her kimonos, her belt with its long ends hanging loosely, and her clogs, either lacquered or edged with brocade, called *pokkuri*. As with a geisha, her skill in being mysterious, her flaunted sensuality, her knowledge of the traditional arts, the whiteness of her make-up, the way she wears her kimono, and her musical voice and calculated simpering, are all signals to a person who wants to seduce, or be seduced by, a young, mysterious beauty.

'At one time the geisha in the
reserved district of Yanagibashi invariably
possessed one of three qualities: beautiful features,
refined manners or intelligence.
Naturally, those endowed with all three were rare;
there still are a few of them.'
  Narushima Ryuhoku (1857–1884), *Ryuko Shinshi*.

▲ Geisha in Shimizu pray and
offer incense during a Buddhist
ceremony. Two of them are
wearing the 'going-out' kimono
of their house, while the third
wears one with a motif of fans,
a symbol of prosperity.

▶ A *maiko* leaves a geisha
house on her way to an
engagement. Her kimono,
with extremely long sleeves,
is decorated with classic
water motifs.

▼ The *pokkuri* worn by
a *maiko*. The lacquered
decoration, showing carp
swimming upstream, forms
a continuous design when
the clogs are placed side
by side.

The sacred phallus

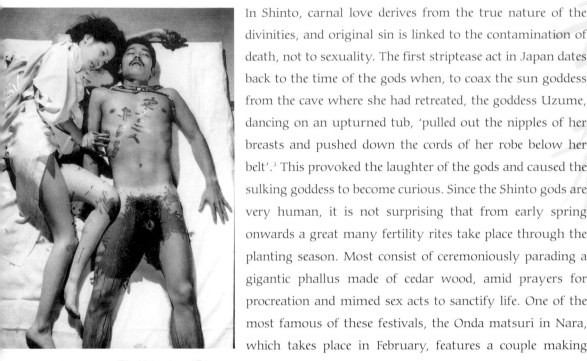

▲ Eiko Matsuda and Tatsuya Fuji in the final scene of *Ai No Corrida/In the Realm of the Senses*, directed by Nagisa Oshima, 1976.

▼ Phallic votive offerings in a shrine in the Hida mountains, central Japan.

▶ A traditional image of prostitution: the young woman holding her kimono belt in her mouth indicates that her robe is no longer acting as the final defender of her virtue.

▶▶ The face's only sign of life and sensuality is represented by the red mouth, reduced to the size of a cherry, the only patch of brightness in the unbroken whiteness of this woman's make-up.

In Shinto, carnal love derives from the true nature of the divinities, and original sin is linked to the contamination of death, not to sexuality. The first striptease act in Japan dates back to the time of the gods when, to coax the sun goddess from the cave where she had retreated, the goddess Uzume, dancing on an upturned tub, 'pulled out the nipples of her breasts and pushed down the cords of her robe below her belt'.[3] This provoked the laughter of the gods and caused the sulking goddess to become curious. Since the Shinto gods are very human, it is not surprising that from early spring onwards a great many fertility rites take place through the planting season. Most consist of ceremoniously parading a gigantic phallus made of cedar wood, amid prayers for procreation and mimed sex acts to sanctify life. One of the most famous of these festivals, the Onda matsuri in Nara, which takes place in February, features a couple making love, the woman wearing the white mask of virginity and the man sporting a red one with a very long nose. The festival of the Tagata shrine, which takes place on 15 March in Komachi, is more spectacular. Young people carry a 5 m (16 ft) phallus to the shrine, while young girls drag along a huge shell, called *hamaguri*, symbolising a vagina. In June, to encourage the rice crop to grow, the Tsuburosashi festival in Niigata stages a seduction dance in which the man waves an enormous wooden phallus attached to his waist. There are many other festivals connected with fertility, not to mention the many natural sights that feature a phallus and vagina, and the many shrines tucked away in the mountains where hundreds of phallus-shaped votive offerings can be found. These are made to bring prosperity to a family or to ask for a good harvest.

3. Félicien Challaye, *Le Japon illustré* [Japan Illustrated], Paris, Librairie Larousse, 1915.

Beautiful
boys

Before Japan opened up to the West at the end of the 19th century, male homosexuality was never the object of moral censure. Quite the opposite, from the Heian period onwards literature was full of it, and of its female counterpart. There was even a long tradition of love for boys, notably among monks, who had no qualms about fondling the page-boys (*chigo*) who were entrusted to the temple, and among warriors, who believed that in a life as fleeting as theirs the love of a man for another man was a higher and more spiritual passion than love felt for a woman. Today, homosexual relations are no more repressed than women's prostitution: they are merely subject to the same restrictions as sexuality in general. However, strangely in a country that does not trouble itself with sexual morality, homosexuality remains an underground practice that often marginalises itself, ranging from the exhibitionism of the transvestites in Tokyo's Golden Gay area and the 300 or so gay establishments in the Shinkuju district, to the discretion, verging on prohibition, among young people who experiment with it before being assimilated into the social fabric of marriage and fidelity. Another characteristic feature of male seduction in Japan is the tendency for men to make themselves more feminine. This usually manifested itself during times of trouble such as the Muromachi period, when the *samurai* of the shogun court, yielding to the influence of the delicately refined Imperial Court, made efforts to dress elegantly, while their wives and daughters wore kimonos with distinctly 'masculine' designs. Today, this feminisation can be observed in the fashions of young men, known as 'peacocks', who wear ostentatious make-up and dress in the most outrageous styles.

▲ A film actor from the Toei company plays a young warrior.

◄ A 1920s film actor in the role of a young samurai.

▼ During the Muromachi period, warriors usually wore clothes whose motifs were more 'feminine' than those of their female companions. This pair of men's trousers, called *hakama*, is from the period when 'dandyism' was common.

化粧
The made-up body

Since the most ancient times, people have resorted to make-up, tattoos and masks to demonstrate the immateriality of the soul and to distinguish themselves from nature. In Japan, this sort of 'grafting of art on to the human body' is pushed to the highest levels of sophistication. In this country, appearance involves more than simple interaction with other people: it weaves a series of highly complex codes with the outer world that are usually filtered through a screen of impassiveness. For this reason, traditional female make-up has no meaning – quite the opposite: it masks the Japanese woman's features and turns her into an abstraction that only acquires meaning in the context of the codes pertaining to a given era. Until quite recently, no respectable woman would have been seen in public without first lightening her skin tone. Even today, a Japanese woman in a kimono will powder her face, avoiding rouge on the cheeks but making her eyelids appear slightly deeper, reducing her eyes to lines and rounding her mouth to resemble a cherry. In this way she is connecting with the past, with the women in the courts of former times – their skin bleached with white lead, their eyebrows shaved off and redrawn higher on their faces, their teeth lacquered black. A woman made up in this style looked just like a goddess. However, on 6 January 1869, a decree by Japan's Imperial Court prohibited this form of make-up from another age. The new taste was for European fashions, and from now on the Meiji emperor would only be seen in a uniform and cocked hat like Napoleon III; at his side, his wife wore a dress with a bustle and carried a silk parasol like the Empress Eugénie.

With the introduction of the bronze mirror, which came from China in the third century, make-up softened the harshness of prehistoric Japanese features. Their faces were coated with red, from the cheeks to the eyes, or marked with tattoos; both men and women were in the habit of lining their eyebrows. In the fifth century, as marriages between clans proliferated, Japanese women discovered coquettishness: the idea of feminine beauty at that time was based on soft features and white skin. The skin was softened using nightingale's droppings and whitened with powdered rice or millet, while camellia oil was used to make the hair shine. Four centuries later, Japanese ladies borrowed their style of make-up from the beauties of the Tang dynasty court in China. This was very distinctive, the whitened face heightened by the use of yellow powder at the roots of the hair, rouge on the cheeks, and beauty-spots at the corners

A *buto* dancer's body make-up.

89

of the mouth and on the forehead. The eyebrows were preferably thick and broad, and were dyed black. This black dye came from chestnut husks, paulownia charcoal, or a mixture of burnt flowers, gold dust, soot and sesame oil. White make-up from this time onwards was made from lead or mercury. During the highly aristocratic Heian period, the taste was for extreme delicacy, and make-up took on a distinctively Japanese character. At this time, the eyebrows became the most important elements of beauty. Their natural state was seen to be hateful, and so 'these horrible caterpillars' were plucked and redrawn, generally higher up the forehead. At first they were in the shape of long, fine crescents, but the most spectacular were broad with softened outlines. They had names such as 'nightingales' or 'soft spring mists'. Later names included 'willow leaves', 'crescent moons', 'butterfly antennae' and 'silkworm cocoons'.

The ladies at court retained these eyebrow styles until the 17th century, while the men heightened theirs with straight, horizontal lines and the boys' eyebrows took the form of oblique lines or round patches. Hair was worn very long – a subject of many poems – emphasising the whiteness of the face which was made up in increasingly thick layers as the style spread among courtesans and dancers. The eyes were drawn out and the mouth reddened and reduced to a minimum. The whole was intended to appear insubstantial and expressionless, for a lady was expected to evince a slight air of detachment and boredom to act as a screen for her feelings. The resulting aesthetic imbued the art of make-up for a long time afterwards. This appearance of melancholic uncertainty, the contrast of sensuality and lack of expression, and the close relationship between beauty and sadness marked the birth of Japanese taste. During the Edo period, the eyebrows were shaved or plucked after marriage as a token of fidelity, or at the birth of the first child. But if a man maintained a 'second wife' or a concubine, this woman retained her eyebrows in their natural state to indicate her lower rank in comparison with the titular wife. Until the beginning of the 20th century, the conventions and materials of make-up barely changed, although around 1880 white lead was superseded by a non-metallic paste, *neri-o-shiroi*, and in subsequent decades there was a general softening of make-up styles in imitation of Western beauties. Even today, Japanese women who value tradition prefer a certain reserve in their dress, and skilful make-up 'whose goal is to pass unnoticed'. However, the geisha and *maiko* still wear the heavy white powder, while *kabuki* actors still enhance the mysterious aspect of their characters by wearing *kumadori*, the highly expressive make-up which is as coded as the masks used in *no* theatre. The make-up worn by an *onnagata*, a male actor playing a female role, idealised women and was relatively close to that of a geisha. Styles used for male roles were much more extravagant, using exaggerated designs to immortalise personality types.

While a *femme fatale* displayed her femininity by means of the *obi* of her kimono, and the *kabuki* or *no* actor specialising in female roles used a mask or make-up to play them, men working in the 'pleasure districts' used tattoos to paint signs of their virility permanently on their body. In the rigidly hierarchical society of the 18th century, decoration with tattoos was already an extreme ornament, which defied the established rules. Intellectuals and artists enthusiastically adopted this subversive art. Novels were published dealing with honourable outlaws who wore tattoos. Since the art of printmaking was then at its height, painters naturally provided the aesthetic language for this new form of dress. During the 19th century, tattoos spread throughout society, especially among firemen, carpenters and craftsmen who worked half-naked, as a mark of courage and as a charm to strengthen their collective bonds, assert their spirit of solidarity and render their body symbolically immortal. However, at the end of the century the government decided to prohibit this image from feudal Japan, and tattoos gradually became the devil's work. Today they are seen as an unhealthy subversion, and must be hidden. Idealising the carnal body by revealing, and at the same time giving it profound meanings – in terms of superstition, provocation or social marginalisation – has made it a private art, the privilege of a class that rejects the safe conformism of a society which, in its eyes, has betrayed its own nature to dress itself up in the ideas of the West. Although it intrigues and excites people, it is only discussed in hushed tones, suggesting a hidden passion for what is forbidden.

The culture of old Japan survives today only in a few genuine manifestations of a traditional world that is disappearing. Far removed from conventional customs such as the tea ceremony, which has adapted to the modern world, tattoos belong to that sometimes secret, parallel world of initiation rites inhabited also by geisha and actors in traditional drama. There are times, however, when the ritual of make-up addresses the modern world, for example in *buto*, the modern style of dance where all-over make-up reconnects the body to primitive forms while placing it firmly in a modern context. This form of drama, described as 'post-Hiroshima', defies aesthetic convention and questions the principles on which society is run. It explores eroticism and violence, agony and ecstasy, the masculine and the feminine – but, like traditional drama, it denies the body's natural state in order to express the body that is absent or has been reconstituted. Here, the convulsive gesture replaces the accepted slowness of *no*. Sometimes the dancers' sculptural forms resemble the *no* costumes or the fixed poses of *kabuki*. When the body is presented resolutely naked, it covers itself with the white of absence, or the ashes of memory.

Black teeth
and tattooed lips

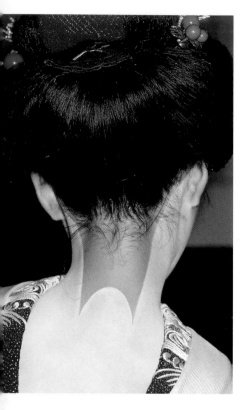

At the beginning of the Heian period, men and women of the nobility began to lacquer their teeth black to 'distinguish themselves from slaves and animals'. Until the 12th century, this practice was very common among the courtesans of the Imperial Court and noblemen going to fight, but it was not until the Kamakura period that it was adopted by the wives of the military elite. The dye – a mixture of iron filings and powdered gallnut mixed with tea or sake – was applied with a brush several times in succession until the desired shade was achieved. The teeth of girls were dyed in this way from the age of ten. As voyageurs at the turn of the last century observed, this custom persisted in the more remote provinces despite the Imperial prohibition of 1869. There, as soon as they were 'in possession' of a husband, wives blackened their teeth, shaved their eyebrows and retreated into their role of spouse. Another strange custom, whose traces could still be seen in the 1930s, was observed by the women of the aboriginal *Ainu* people on the island of Hokkaido, whose menfolk had abundant facial hair. They felt their beauty was enhanced by permanently adorning their upper lips with a sort of broad moustache, which was tattooed on their face from the age of 13 or 14. Today, thanks to the influence of international fashion, it is not unusual to see Japanese women with black or very dark lipstick and matching nail varnish. This kind of make-up has no connection with the black sported by the little girls, dressed in red, who play the roles of demons in certain plays. It is done simply as a memory of the black teeth of princesses from the days of legend and, as their make-up did, it adorns a face rendered enigmatic by white make-up.

◀ The special make-up on the nape of a *maiko*. The area of skin left uncovered, which is regarded as highly erotic, also keeps the chignon from touching the make-up.

▼ *Ainu* women as they could be seen in the early years of the last century, with a kind of moustache tattooed on their upper lips.

▶ Make-up in the style chosen by 14th-century princesses, with the eyebrows shaved and painted higher on the face, in the shape of clouds.

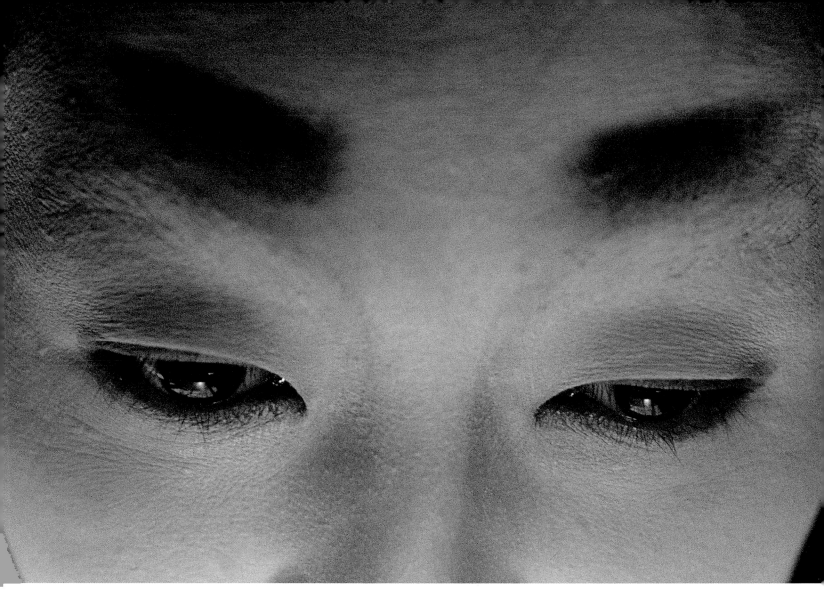

▲ Make-up in the style of
a 14th-century princess.
At that time no expression
could be allowed to show
through on the face of a
person of noble birth.

◄ Unlike their elders,
young girls today use slightly
stronger hues in their make-up,
at the expense of whiteness.
As in the past, however, the
ideal make-up should not be
noticeable.

'Exquisite and strange,
with the look of a cold goddess
gazing inwards,
gazing beyond,
gazing who knows where.'
Pierre Loti.

The exquisite make-up of the geisha

A geisha begins her toilet by applying two scented oils, one of which is used to flatten her eyebrows, before she coats herself with the *neri-o-shiroi* white make-up, which she applies in a set order: first on the cheeks, then on the neck, the chin, and finally on the central part of the face, which has been carefully shaved to 'hold' the make-up better. She then puts some rouge on her forehead, eyelids and the sides of her nose, and then gives the whole a matt finish with a powder called *kona-o-shiroi*. She draws the black lines of the eyebrows in, highlights the outline of the eyes in red to make the iris appear lighter and the eye cavity deeper, and blackens her eyelashes. She completes her make-up by applying red to her lips to make her mouth appear smaller, and partly covers the fleshier lower lip with white. Having finished her face, the geisha concentrates on making up her neck, to show off her nape to advantage. This too is carefully whitened, but leaves bare the three triangles of skin known as *sambon-ashi* ('the three legs'). A *maiko* will have only two 'legs' on her nape. In this way the grain of the skin is made to look as transparent as possible, with the faintest blue veining – an invitation to eroticism, hinting at the secrets of a forbidden intimacy. This elegant quirk was formerly used by courtesans and their apprentices to distinguish themselves from lower-class prostitutes, who did not bother with such subtleties. After spending an hour putting on her heavy kimono, pushing back its collar to attract glances, and putting the finishing touches to her complex hairstyle to make sure that not a hair will be out of place when she dances, the geisha or *maiko* slips on her high clogs and makes her way to her engagement, where her dress and talents will be fully appreciated.

◄ Utamaro, *White Make-up*, about 1795. Musée Guimet, Paris.

▼ A *maiko* applies the scented oil that is the base of her make-up.

► A *maiko* applies the *neri-o-shiroi* to her neck. She will need an assistant to whiten her nape and trace the 'legs' of bare skin at the hairline.

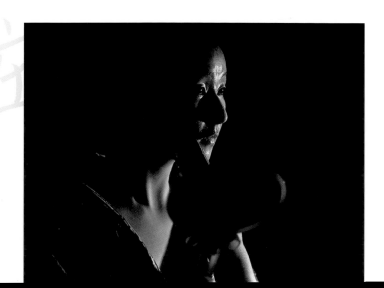

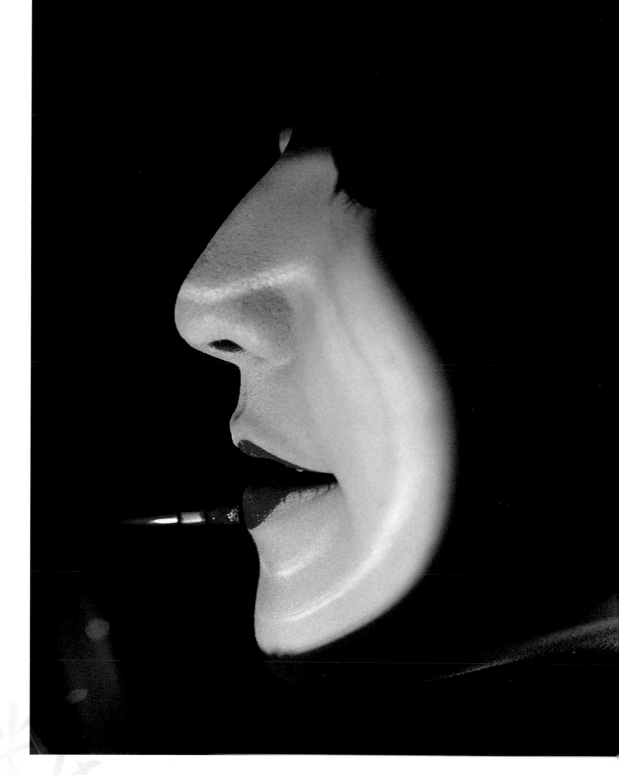

◄ A *maiko* retouches the make-up on her eyebrows.

► The made-up face of a geisha is a mask rather like those used in *no* theatre. It plays its part using the same effects and the same ambiguity.

'Although one of them may look pretty,
she owes her beauty to the artifice of powder,
rouge and luxurious kimonos.
Such devices were once scorned by real geisha,
who left them to ordinary courtesans.
They took a pride in their faces free from make-up
and their dress consisting of kimonos in discreet
tones and designs.'
    Narushima Ryuhoku (1857–1884), *Ryuko Shinshi*.

Stylised make-up
in kabuki theatre

Kumadori make-up was reputedly invented in the 17th century by the actor Ichikawa Danjuro, when he painted his body red to play the part of a god. The hues used in this expressive form of make-up are precisely worked out, just like the costumes of *kabuki*. They are not intended to accentuate physical attributes or convey emotions, but to portray stereotyped characters and feelings. All the main characters who are considered noble and good, and all the women, wear white make-up on their faces, hands and feet. Rogues, enemies and demons are distinguished from these benevolent characters by a toned foundation, generally dark red, or by blue highlights applied in broad waves. As for lower-class people, their make-up is 'flesh-toned'. There are strict conventions governing the various types of mouth, nose, eyes, eyebrows and ears, and their relationship with the essence of a character. The actor is really building up a mask on his face when he 'hollows out the shadows' of his make-up with shaded lines. While black is used to accentuate the features, eyebrows, creases of bitterness and signs of age, red is used to emphasise the features of positive characters, especially the lower eyelid and the outer edge of the eyes, while blue does the same job with negative characters. As in *no* theatre, where the character is created through the mask, in *kabuki* it emerges gradually through the application of *kumadori*. The actor effaces his own personality, first by spreading white over his entire face, and then by using a finger and brush to draw in the lines which reveal the intensity of a hero, the sensuality of a woman, the malevolence of a traitor or the mystery of a god.

▶ The *kabuki* actor Ichikawa Ennosuke III in the role of Kurozuka, standing behind a monk carrying out an exorcism.

▼ A *kabuki* scene portraying the life of the divine hero Yamato Takeru. Thanks to the *kumadori* make-up, the characters' ages, personalities and social roles are clearly defined.

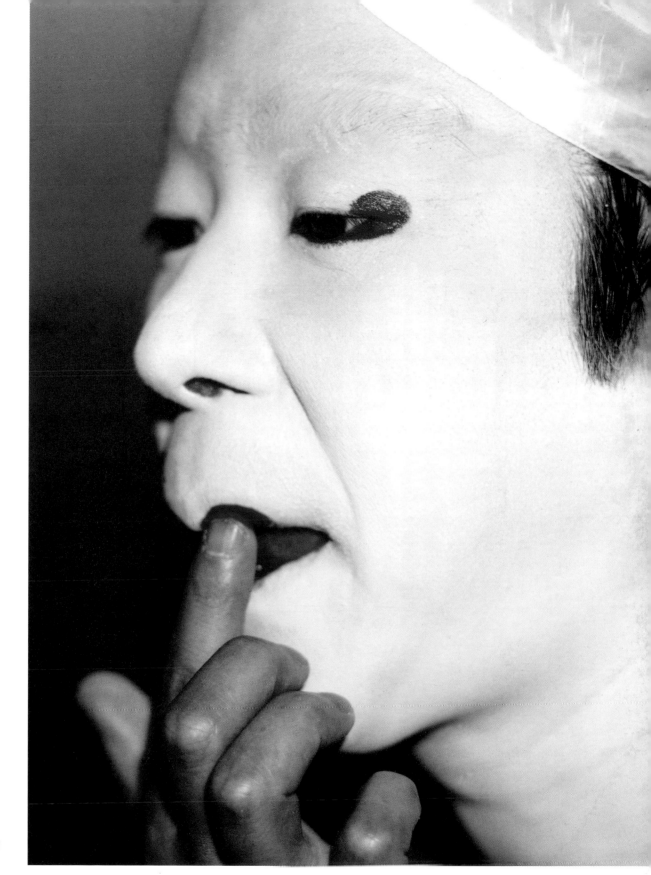

◀ The *kabuki* actor
Nakamura Shibajaku VII
as a 'butterfly'.

▶ The actor Ichikawa
Ennosuke III making himself
up as a woman.

'The traditional arts are ambiguous,
because it is in that very ambiguity
that reality is to be found.'
Baba Akiko
Poet and actress, *No* theatre.

▲ A young man displays his tattoo of the fire god Fudo Myo-o on his back.

▶ A tattooed man drinks at a fountain. When displaying their 'brocade skin', tattooed men wear the traditional *fundoshi* loincloth.

An art of flesh and blood

Tattooing, known as *irezumi* or *horimono*, is a kimono made of flesh and blood, which the wearer dons for life to bring good fortune, guard against illness and demonstrate his courage. Apart from its subversive power and the magical influence its designs may have on others, tattoo is said to be the prerogative of gangsters, the *yakuza*; a concept that is enough to conjure up the smell of sulphur and malevolence, blood and suffering. Tattooing is a living and moving work of art, like a screen, a kimono or a scroll painting. It is never a decoration, but an art practised by masters who sign their creations with pseudonyms, as artists who produced prints once did. The term 'engraving' is used in preference to 'painting' to describe this method of adorning the body. This glorification of the flesh is not achieved without violence, although since the 1930s cocaine has sometimes been used as an anaesthetic by mixing it with the ink. The typically Japanese techniques of 'downy' *hanebori* and the *bokashibori* method of shading hues are extremely painful, especially when they use cinnabar (for red), yellow and green. From an iconographic point of view, the repertoire of tattooing is essentially Buddhist, since Shinto rejects all defilement, especially that of the blood. Gods and legendary heroes account for much of that repertoire, and express the masculine virtues of tenacity, strength, courage and loyalty in their symbolic designs: cherry blossoms, peonies, clouds, lightning, pine needles, maple leaves and water motifs, which also appear on the kimonos of geisha. Classic themes from the animal world include the longevity of the crane, the bravery of the carp, the power of the tiger and the immortality of the dragon.

武士
Image
and the body

The body is a figment of the imagination, a fiction. Each time it is portrayed, in words or images, we constantly reinvent it. This is even more true when we idealise the bodies of an entire people on the basis of a few isolated images – such as the geisha, *yakuza* or samurai – which we elevate to the rank of absolute truths. To this body we attach the notion of beauty, whether real, supposed or desired, and we shrink from revealing the simple truth of its form. All beauty is thus a fantasy, and to present it as a model is to lie. Sometimes, however, we need to give substance to the unknown forces of nature: the bodies of gods, whether beautiful or terrifying, must be invented in order to be worshipped. Conversely, reality needs to be embellished: the boorish soldier must become a hero, and the courtesan a geisha, if a nation is to unite around a single ideal – especially when that nation is itself the greatest of fictions, as symbolised by the cult of the emperor. There are times, though, when other models interfere: fashions are eager for new blood, the perennial desire for East and West. In Japan, the fiction still consists of believing in the mirage of the stars, in divination, in superstitions – of being convinced that a name describes a person, and that it is enough to change it at each stage of one's life to achieve a higher destiny.

Images of the body began with the creation of the world, and the idea that the first Japanese child was the first of Japan's islands. From the beginning, all Japanese people benefit from a single body – called Japan – to which they owe their existence. They venerate its invisible forces, sometimes giving them substance as a mask, a palanquin, a white horse, a doll, a mirror or a sacred page boy. When the divine actually takes on a human form, it is in the person of the emperor. He is descended from the sun goddess, and is as inviolable as the ground on which his throne stands. The Japanese empire is thus totally identified with its Imperial family. In the 1870s, when the young Meiji emperor became the first ruler to shed the aura of an invisible divinity, the people still looked at the ground when he was passing, fearing they would be struck down by the royal star. When Hirohito, under US pressure, renounced his divine status in 1945, he was obliged to announce this himself, on the radio. This act – incomprehensible to most Japanese – caused many of his subjects to commit suicide as a respectful expression of disagreement with the fallen god, without the slightest intention (unlike the young kamikaze who had just given their lives for Japan the Great) of earning the most trifling honour by this terrible act.

Offerings placed in the hollow of a tree. Because of its peculiar shape, the tree is considered sacred and is therefore the dwelling-place of a spirit of nature.

Since Japan had never been invaded in its history, the Japanese never had cause to modify the forms inherited from their gods: at most, they could evolve their ideals of beauty over centuries. Each age had its own, and each class its criteria for defining it, leaving painters, print engravers and actors the task of creating a multitude of models. Thus, in the Heian period, women were reduced to cascades of hair and sumptuous dresses – a mere idea of a woman, their eyes invisible, their mouths silent. It was not until the 17th century that 'beautiful women' appeared in painting, but these were the wives or daughters of town-dwellers, prostitutes or *kabuki* actors. Artists of this period had a keen interest in feminine beauty: some preferred the aristocratic type, with a long, delicate face, others the daughters of common people, with round, fresh cheeks. Apart from their seductive black hair and the whiteness of their skin, everyone appreciated these young girls' fine, translucent skin, thick eyebrows set far apart, long nose, small mouth drawn like two petals of a flower side by side, their curving nape, long, slender fingers and well-arched feet. The most beautiful 'invented' women of the Edo period came from the brushes of three great lovers of the sensual: Harunobu, Kiyonaga and Utamaro. The beauties painted by Harunobu are like lilies, with slender bodies, devoid of breasts or hips, and relatively small heads. Those by Kiyonaga, in their sumptuous kimonos, are more 'womanly', while Utamaro's courtesans are more sensual, with their gracefully elongated bodies, often partly unclothed. However, all these ideal women's expressive features – the eyes, nose and mouth – are still reduced to mere representations: they reveal nothing of these beauties' inner thoughts.

The warrior's body is another Japanese convention. For the foreigner as much as for the Japanese, it replaces the real with the imaginary. Originally, the samurai, 'he who serves', became in the eyes of the West a perfect warrior, innately noble and master of himself in any situation, someone who, as the saying goes, 'serenely takes a toothpick to his mouth even when he has nothing to eat'. For the Japanese this model has been rediscovered, after a long period of oblivion, as a truly national one. But unlike Westerners, who are enthusiastic about fighting prowess, the Japanese prefer to stress the purity of a man who has sworn only one oath: to be ready to die at all times. 'At that time a samurai prepared himself every morning. He shaved the front of his head, smoothed and scented his knot of hair, cut his fingernails and toenails, and polished them.'[4] He also took great care of his weapons and clothing. This attention to his appearance was not aimed to seduce, but was a mark of respect for the opponent who would strike him down. Well before the Edo period, the rules of knightly discipline recommended that a warrior should not go into battle without first applying perfume, lacquering his teeth and adding pink to his cheeks, so as not to upset the enemy who would decapitate him. When committing *seppuku*, Mishima explains, 'the code which prohibited a man from disgracing himself in front of an enemy demanded that he should beautify himself just before death, taking care to preserve the appearance of vigorous life'.[5] This fine ideal of martial glory disappeared when the carrying of swords was banned in 1876.

As in feudal times, the birth of a child causes much family speculation about its future. In a society that emphasises the group above the individual, a name is more important than its bearer, especially if the bearer is a boy. It must therefore be chosen with care, and divination must be used to establish the child's destiny. The Chinese signs of the zodiac play a great part in the lives of the Japanese, who frequently consult fortune-tellers to know what their future holds. They are very suspicious, for example, of girls born in the year of the fire horse: these have very little chance of marrying since they reputedly consume their husbands. Today, however, an individual's name is eclipsed by an even greater fiction, which surpasses it: business. Since most Japanese belong to the same social class and have similar levels of professional qualification, the individual is 'he who serves', and has no value except in relation to his or her employer. Thus on a business card – the true proof of social status – the name of the company comes first, followed by a person's job title, with their name in last place. In a country where for a long time behaviour and appearances were strictly codified, dress too was a means of expressing social values and, despite occasional influences upon it during the course of history, only the kimono proved really suited to the Japanese convention of 'shapeless' forms and gestures. The adoption of Western dress from the Meiji period onwards was a way of breaking the old order and pursuing the dream of Westernisation. But it was not until the 1950s that a truly Japanese type of Western-style dress appeared, consciously aimed at improving people's condition by making them aware of their bodies as much as of their personalities. References to the West in modern Japanese criteria of beauty are far more subtle than they were at the beginning of the 20th century. They no longer seek to imitate behaviour and forms directly, for example through the use of plastic surgery to widen the eyes and lengthen the nose, but instead use the Western model to help define an 'authentic' modern Japanese identity. Thus 'a white person in an advertisement does not really exist: that person is an idealised representation of a Japanese. He or she is not a white person at all but an "ideal Japanese". We do not resort to white people as such, but to those who are closest to the ideal Japanese figure.'[6]

4. Yamamoto Tsunemoto, 'Hagakure' in Mishima Yukio, Le japon moderne et l'éthique samourai [The Samurai Ethic and Modern Japan], Paris, Gallimard, 'Arcades' series, 1985.
5. Mishima Yukio, Le japon moderne et l'éthique samourai [The Samurai Ethic and Modern Japan], op cit.
6. Kozakai Toshiaki, Ovni No. 233, 15 March 1989.

The invisible presence of the gods

◀ Inari the fox, originally a messenger from the god of rice, is especially worshipped for its own sake among shopkeepers, and many shrines are dedicated to it.

▼ The rocks of Futami-ga-ura, near Ise, linked together by the sacred rope of marriage.

▶ Sumo wrestlers, whose earthly bouts recall the titanic struggles of the gods, generally sign themselves with a handprint placed above their calligraphic name, as on this ex-voto from the Shorinzan Daruma-ji, Takasaki.

By definition, the Shinto gods (*kami*) are invisible to humans and only prove their existence through phenomena assumed to reveal their presence, such as quirks of the weather and good or bad harvests, and others that indicate their dwelling places, such as rocks, trees and mountain peaks. Some of these places have an immanent spirit, such as Mount Fuji. People nevertheless need to visualise these gods, and to give them human characteristics. Thus the two famous rocks of Futami-ga-ura, linked by a rope, are married, and the whistling of the wind in the forests is simply the chattering of trees talking to each other. There are many divinities, some of which came into existence in an extraordinary way, but above them rule three great divinities born of the ablutions which the god Izanagi was obliged to perform when he emerged from the underworld. When he cleaned his nose, his right eye and then his left, he brought into being, respectively, Susano-o, the impetuous god of storms who reigns over the ocean; Tsuki, the goddess responsible for the moons who governs the realm of the night, and Amaterasu, the luminous sun goddess who lights the world. The *kami* govern everything that exists in the three worlds: the High Plains of the heavens, the Land of Reeds in the middle, where humans live, and the Land of Yomi, the underworld of the dead. Crops such as rice, millet, wheat, red beans and soya, and also silkworms, are the source of agriculture and represent life that dies and is unceasingly reborn. They are derived from the divine, and more precisely they sprang from the body of a divinity who was killed on the High Plains. Plants are accorded a soul, and priests make offerings to them at sowing time. The emperor himself supervises the celebration of the rice-planting rite at the great shrine of Ise.

▲ A representation of the god of thunder at the Kamigamo-jinja, Kyoto. When the shrine was being consecrated, lightning split a pine on the hilltop – an event represented by two pine needles inserted into a pile of sand.

◀ The passage of sacred arches, *torii*, made as votive offerings to the divinity Inari at the great shrine of Fushimi, near Kyoto.

'I do not know what sacred thing lurks here,
yet I am weeping tears of gratitude.'
Saigyo, 10th-century poet.

Ashamed of
their bodies

It was only at the end of the 19th century that the Japanese began to blush at the shape of their bodies, finding them poorly suited to the European dress so prized at the time. They felt their heads were too large, their shoulders too narrow, their chests too long, their arms and legs too short, and their calves and ankles too thick. Men even started complaining that they did not have enough body hair – while at the same time despising the 'hairy' Chinese, the hirsute *Ainu* and bearded foreigners. Young Japanese women of the time became obsessed by the idea that the Western body was more attractive than their own, and dreamed of having longer, more slender limbs, a bigger bust, and finer, straighter legs. Although their bodies were a reflection of the past, their evolution was seen as a means of change, a proof of the new nation's modernity. Japanese women wanted to look like the Western women portrayed on the prints of the time. Their husbands, however, thought that these prints were angular, bony, ungainly and pretentious, whereas in contrast a Japanese woman in her kimono was modest and extremely pretty: 'It is through the mouths of its women that Japan smiles at foreigners; through their eyes it cajoles and bewitches them ...' wrote Ludovic Nadeau.[7] Griffis added: 'The temptations this country offers are fearsome: many have succumbed who would have been unmoved at home. In fact, few Europeans, apart from priests and missionaries, have not erred.'[8] Each dreamed of an imaginary body that could replace their own. Since that time, the body shape of Japanese people has changed – sport, changes in diet and different living conditions and furniture being mainly responsible. Japanese women need envy their Western sisters no longer.

◄ The *buto* dancer Carlotta Ikeda expresses maximum bodily tension. Her body is typical of the Japanese body shape.

▼ Japanese spectators watch projections of idealised Western bodies on screens in an exhibition hall in Tsukuba science city.

▶▶ Shinto divinities, unlike those of Buddhism, are depicted only very rarely. The divine characters represented in the *kabuki* play *Yamato Takeru* are dressed in white to indicate that they belong to the world of the heavens.

7. Ludovic Nadeau, 'Le Japon moderne' [Modern Japan] in *Le Japon illustré* [Japan Illustrated], Librairie Larousse, Paris, 1915.
8. Griffis, 'Verbeck of Japan' in *Le Japon illustré*, op cit.

The samurai code of honour

▲ A 1920s film actor plays a young samurai of the Muromachi period.

▼ Armour is not only the warrior's second skin, but a body in its own right designed to terrify the enemy.

▶ An actor of the Toei film company plays a *ronin*, a samurai without a master. His situation is indicated by the knot of hair pulled towards the front, and by the fact that the hair on his upper forehead has not been shaved.

The *Hagakure*, a didactic work aimed at 18th-century samurai, asserted that a man who did not exude serenity, dignity and calm could not appear good-looking. Anyone who was to achieve this measure of self-control needed to be reserved, even austere and rigorous, but always loyal, just and respectful of others. These martial virtues of simplicity and loyalty were later organised into what came to be known as the *bushido*, the 'way of the warrior'. This famous code of honour of the samurai, forged from Zen Buddhism and Confucianism, set out the mutual duties of rulers and their vassals. It taught not only how to develop courage and physical qualities, but also how to behave with superiors: it advocated honesty, generosity, selflessness and contempt for death. The essence of *bushido* survives today only in a diminished form, in the practice of martial arts – but in the Second World War it still inspired the young *kamikaze* who wore the 'band of determination' on their foreheads, marked with the Imperial sun. When a man today identifies with the myth of the samurai, he is first and foremost claiming the secular inheritance of the warrior's social rank, strength and supremacy – as conveyed by his feet planted firmly on the ground, his proud bearing, his belly thrust forward, back straight, head held high. Like his model, he speaks extremely concisely in a deep voice, very different from the mellifluous tones of a woman. The writer Mishima Yukio – the last person to have genuinely preached this code, taking it as far as his own *seppuku* – asserted: 'If we place such a high value on the dignity of life, how can we not place an equally high value on the dignity of death? Death can never be described as futile.'[9]

9. Mishima Yukio, *Le Japon moderne et l'éthique samurai* [The Samurai Ethic and Modern Japan], op. cit.

'A sword
that does not respond
in an instant
is not a sword.'
Miyamoto Musashi,
17th century.

◄ Lacquered armour mask, 16th century.

▲ Since a sword was regarded as the samurai's alter ego, he took great care to choose the various elements of the handle to reflect his personality, like this knob on the end of the hilt.

► Archers trained in shooting from horseback, dressed in hunting costumes of the feudal period, walk towards the incense fountain in the Senso-ji temple, Tokyo.

Fashion: a dialogue with the West

During the 1960s street fashion, infatuated with the US, drove a number of designers to draw on the wellspring of haute couture and make their début in the big Western fashion houses. These pioneers, such as Issey Miyake, Yoji Yamamoto and Rei Kawakubo, set fashion free by revolutionising the very laws of style. Thanks to them, clothing came in that was designed to bring the body to life rather than to emphasise its forms or simply to cover it. To mock and challenge convention, the time-honoured contrast between female and male fashion was left behind, and notions of style and elegance were rejected in a 'luxurious tramp' style, the 'zero degree of clothing', consisting of deconstructed, loose-fitting and sometimes torn garments. At the beginning of the 1980s, a decade after Kenzo had opened the first Japanese boutique in Paris, fashion became a means of communication, a sign of intelligence. Freedom and success were expressed through appearance, and brand image was no longer the concern only of commercial companies alone but of consumers themselves. Although the Japanese body shape was approaching Western standards, Japanese fashion, rejecting all 'Greek' idealisations of the body, instead favoured functional clothes that allowed the space between the body and the material to come to life – 'tools for living' that aimed for psychological as much as physical comfort. During the following decade a third wave of designers rediscovered sensuality and natural, or idealised femininity, and close-fitting clothes again made their appearance. Today, freed from Western dictates, Japanese fashion sees itself as international and has gained acceptance not just in Asia but in the West as well.

▼ Issey Miyake, collection 2001.

▶ Young girls in Tokyo's fashionable Harajuku district.

▶▶ Issey Miyake, Ode to Nuba collection, 1976 – a tribute to the work of the photographer Leni Riefenstahl on the Nuba people.

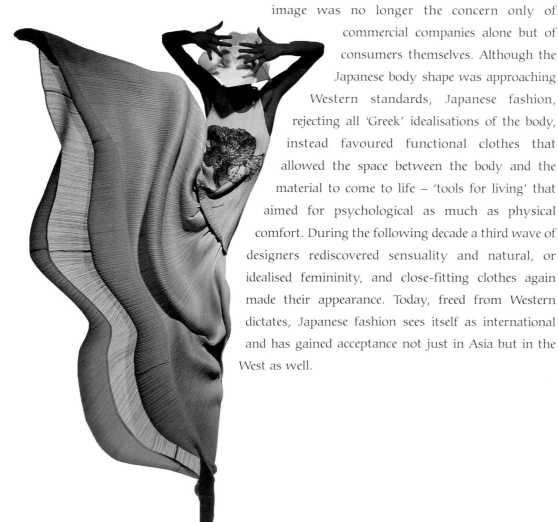

The art of
choosing a name

◀ After nightfall fortune-tellers, astrologers, palmists and other soothsayers set out their stalls in the streets and await their customers by the light of a lantern.

▼ The Japanese believe in the signs of the Chinese zodiac, based on a 12-year cycle. Every year, the astrological sign is used to make numerous good luck charms, such as these dragons in samurai costume.

▶ Warriors in armour at the Nomaoi *matsuri* festival in Soma. The standards, in the hues of feudal clans, do not only help recognition on the battlefield but also indicate that an individual only exists as part of a group.

It used to be the custom to give a newborn child a name which was then discarded at the age of about 15, when the child was no longer a minor. Since the person's new name would be highly intimate, it often carried a sort of taboo, and it was customary to mask it with a large number of nicknames, epithets and pseudonyms. This adult name was often changed, on average about ten times, at each important stage of a person's life, particularly in craft and artistic circles. Finally, at their funeral, a person received a posthumous name, which the Buddhist monk chose taking into account their age, sex, rank and the sect to which they belonged. Today it is still common to choose a child's baptismal name by resorting to divination. This is done by adding up the number of brushstrokes required to write a name's ideograms, and so arriving at a figure considered lucky, neutral or unlucky. Since the family name cannot be changed, it is common to seek out a specialised fortune-teller to decide on a first name whose ideograms, when added to those of the family name, give an auspicious figure. Other methods of divination include palmistry (reading the lines of the hand or foot), analysis of the physiognomy, the 'science' of dreams, reading Chinese diagrams and consulting the oracles in a Shinto shrine. Traditionally, too, certain ages are thought to be unlucky. Men or women who have reached those ages must be especially careful to perform all their religious duties to ward off ill-luck. On the other hand, the 61st year, coming at the end of a zodiacal cycle, is celebrated with great solemnity because it is thought to be a second birth.

▲ A tile in the shape of a Buddhist demon, said to protect buildings from evil influences.

◀ The *tengu* is a sort of spirit of Buddhist legend and Japanese folklore which likes to play unpleasant tricks on humans. Some are featured with a beak and a bird's wings; others, such as this one, have a long phallic nose.

'They deigned to pursue, in a divine pursuit,
the wild divinities of the land thus bestowed;
and they deigned to expel them, in a divine expulsion;
and they silenced the rocks, the tree trunks, and even the
tiniest blades of grass, which had had the gift of speech;
and, dispatching him from the heavenly seat of the rocks,
clearing a path, powerfully parting a way through the
celestial clouds folded eight times upon themselves,
respectfully they brought him down and bestowed
this land upon him.'

Shinto ritual from the *Great Purification of the
Last Day of the Humid Moon* (Michel Revon, *Anthologie
de la littérature japonaise* [Anthology of Japanese Literature].

祭典

The festive body

The Japanese live in close symbiosis with nature, even when it becomes destructive. Feasts of thanksgiving, collective prayers and countless festivals bear witness to the spiritual, even unconscious power that the Japanese people attribute to nature and therefore to its gods. These gods, who between them guarantee the immutable order of things, also drive humans to the wild religious festivals called *matsuri*. In the distant past, the gods themselves felt the need to hold a festival – the first of its kind – when they had to persuade the sun goddess to end her isolation, creating the fabric for her to cover herself and improperly reveal herself, and inventing dance, music and intoxication. For a Japanese, a festival is a time of total gaiety, when the body is freed from all the duties and conventions of everyday life, which are among the most restrictive in the world. The gods love the vitality of young people, the movement of the crowd, the elegance of dance steps, the singing of young girls, the boys' drums, the merriment of the not-so-young and the fond reserve of the elderly. This provides humans with many opportunities to please them. Since humans are impure, the *matsuri* is by definition also a means of purification, whose rites must be scrupulously observed to safeguard the harmony of the world. It is a strange, divine contradiction to mix respectful worship with these highly permissive outbursts. But what complicity there is between the gods and humans; between them they can vanquish evil spirits, malevolent demons and bad thoughts. A festival must above all be a quest for happiness and fertility. For this reason, most *matsuri* are connected with agriculture and more specifically with the sowing, planting out and harvesting of rice. Since crops are at greatest risk in summer, because of typhoons, droughts and diseases, the biggest festivals of the year – with the exception of those at New Year – are held during that season.

It is said that at least one festival takes place every day in Japan, in honour of its 'eight million gods'. Some are very exclusive, involving only a local divinity in a small village shrine; others are huge events attended by thousands from all over the country. They combine old traditions, costumes, music and ancient religious rituals with the wildest merrymaking. Formerly, festival dates were set according to the lunar calendar. The days of the new moon and its two quarters were regarded as separate from the other days of the month; they were thought to be lucky days and commemorative celebrations were always planned for them. Today these events are gradually losing

A page boy at the Gion festival in Kyoto. Voted the year's best-behaved child, the little *chigo* becomes, for the duration of the festival, the divinity's human representative.

their religious character and, as they turn into commercial folk festivals, generally fall on fixed dates. Festivals may be held to give thanks to the guardian divinity of a place or to commemorate an event in local life, an act of bravery by a local hero, a victory or a scourge. Others embrace the entire country, such as those connected to farming, festivals of the seasons which celebrate plants coming into bloom and attract crowds of enthusiasts, and commemorative festivals with processions of floats, people on horseback, princesses and samurai. There are also the festivals marking the 'opening' and 'closing' of the season for climbing Mount Fuji; the latter, held on the last day of August, is the occasion for a spectacular torch-lit procession down the mountain which can be seen for miles around.

The most endearing celebrations are those involving children: the festival of the ages, the festival of girls and the festival of boys. Each of these is a solemn occasion, for the children pay their respects to their family's tutelary god at the shrine nearest their home. The girls' festival, also called the 'festival of peach-trees' or 'festival of dolls' is held on 3 March. On that day, little girls invite their friends, drink tea and eat cakes before dolls from the ancient Imperial Court arranged on a platform hung with red cloth. On 5 May, the boys' festival, young boys take a bath of iris leaves, which are shaped like swords, to imbue them with a warrior spirit and give them strength and health. They then receive their friends before the platform where a replica suit of armour is displayed while, up on the roof of the house, windsocks shaped like carp are hoisted – because that fish is the perfect symbol of courage. Buddhism, introduced to Japan in the sixth century, has its own festivals such as *o-bon*, also known as the 'festival of lanterns', when the souls of ancestors are welcomed back and cared for over three days, to allow them to share the joy of humans. Buddhism also marks the anniversaries of gods and monks who founded sects.

The idea behind a festival is to invite the gods down to earth in order to benefit from their supernatural power. The most important moment of a *matsuri* is the *naorai*, during which the assembled people take time to meditate and purify their thoughts, pray for better harvests, fight off illness and hope for a better life. A festival has three sections. First, the god is invited to come and reside temporarily in its earthly dwelling. For this to happen, the shrine, priests and other participants are first purified, then the doors are opened to the place where the god is to be welcomed. The senior priest makes a welcome speech and offers gifts to the divinity, such as flowers, money, food and *sake*. The second part of the *matsuri* is the most spectacular: the local young people parade the divinity in a palanquin resembling a miniature shrine. Dances and music are performed as offerings to the divine visitor, as well as various other performances, such as archery and martial arts tournaments. The final part of the *matsuri* is when the gods are respectfully invited to return to the heavens and the ceremony concludes with the clearing of the table bearing the offerings.

While the *matsuri* is a way of making contact with the gods, sport – whether Western or traditional – is also an opportunity to celebrate the body. Western sports were introduced to Japan when it opened up to the West at the beginning of the Meiji period – as can be seen in a print of 1876 showing boys and girls in kimonos exercising with weights in one of Japan's first primary schools. Two years later, a gymnastics institute was set up to start physical exercise in schools; fifty years later, in these same schools, children were regularly being treated with ultra-violet and infra-red rays to improve their physical condition. In the meantime, Western teachers working in Japan, and students returning from study trips abroad, had introduced the idea that the Japanese body shape, so different from that of Westerners, needed to be improved. Foreign sports were a symbol of Meiji modernity, but remained a luxury until Kano Jigoro, who devised judo in 1882, advocated proper physical education. Thanks to him, sport was developed throughout the educational system, with special emphasis placed on judo, kendo, Zen archery, gymnastics and baseball. All modern sports are practised in Japan today, but the three main ones are baseball, which is played from childhood well into adulthood, golf (limited almost entirely to practice) and sumo, which is above all a televised sport. Baseball, called *yakyu* in Japan, was the first to be introduced, in 1873; it was played initially among students, before the formation of the two professional leagues whose tournaments are followed by millions of fans today. Golf, introduced in 1903, only became popular from the 1950s onwards; but the pleasure of playing on one of the country's 600 superb courses is the preserve of professionals and wealthy businessmen. As for sumo, it excites the fiercest passions and has generated a star system among the huge wrestlers who re-create in the ring the struggle between two Shinto divinities for control of the province of Izumo. Apart from sumo, which is centuries old, martial arts now attract few followers, but for Westerners they remain one of the enduring images of Japan because of the 'oriental' wisdom they are supposed to develop in their practitioners.

▶▶ Fishing allows the Japanese to indulge their love of leisure and taste for uniforms. Enthusiasts of all sports tend to dress and buy equipment like that of the professionals.

Festive frenzy

In all religions of the world, people feel the need to leave the confines of their bodies in order to talk to the gods. The dizziness of a trance, the mind-numbing effect of competition, the excitement of dancing and the frenzy of making an extreme effort all converge at that point when the physiological being disconnects from reality and becomes oblivious to the limits of the body. This supreme abandonment of the self can be seen when a divinity pays a visit to humans, and young people filled with passion carry the *mikoshi*, a heavy sacred palanquin in which the divinity temporarily resides. Sometimes, during one of these divine visits, several *mikoshi* find themselves in competition. The teams may then clash violently, as if the gods themselves were fighting each other to reach the shrine first. Usually, however, the *mikoshi* parades are peaceful and consist of passing through a crowd, crossing a river or immersion in the sea. In Tokyo, the Kanda and Sanja *matsuri* spring festivals in Tokyo bring together 65 and 100 palanquins respectively in a joyous uproar, each carried by bearers dressed in a festival jacket displaying a corporate logo, and wearing headbands called *hachimaki* on their foreheads. Some of the palanquins are enormous and require large numbers of bearers. So too are the huge lanterns, called *nebuta*, at the summer festivals in northern Japan, and the floats at the Gion festival in Kyoto, some of which weigh more than a tonne and need 20 people to haul them along. This frenzy of the body can also be seen in most of the festivals of purification by water or fire, as well as in the frenetic beating of festival drums. In all of these, the participants' 'divine intoxication' creates an illusion of total communion with the gods.

◀ Most of the big summer festivals in northern Japan are festivals of lanterns, like the Kanto *matsuri* in Akita. Those who take part in the procession have to balance impressive displays of lanterns in their hands.

▼ The *mikoshi* makes its appearance. This is the sacred palanquin in which a divinity temporarily resides when paying a visit to humans to take part in their celebrations.

▶ One of the special features of the Shizuoka festival is the presence of traditional firework makers. Their bamboo tubes are packed with gunpowder and tightly bound with cord to prevent them exploding, but the bursts of blazing ashes are still extremely dangerous, and assistants constantly spray the participants with water.

▶▶ Young girls acting as ladies of the Muromachi Court at the festival of the Sumiyoshi shrine near Osaka.

Children's festivals

祭典

On 15 November, all children who have reached the age of three, five and seven during the year take part in the celebration of *shichi-go-san* to bring the gods' good grace upon themselves. For this occasion they put on their best finery. Formerly, the hair of three-year-old girls was combed for the first time on this day, and boys' hair was allowed to grow longer. The occasion also celebrated the children's discarding of baby clothes in favour of normal children's clothes; the youngsters could then visit shrines and take part in festivals. At the age of five, boys would sit enthroned on a *go* board, symbol of the battlefield, to celebrate donning a warrior's trousers. Two years later they would receive their first ceremonial jacket, signifying that they were authorised to honour the gods regularly, while at the same age girls would mark the 'abolition of the fixed fastening', the device which had hitherto secured their kimono, and went on to 'take the belt'. This new *obi* was still very narrow but little girls, then as now, wore this real woman's accessory with pride. In Japan, the seventh birthday was a crucial date, for then a child would achieve the status of a full family member, which brought with it the right to an adult's funeral. It was not until the age of 13, however, that a child truly became a member of society. Then at New Year, children were presented with their first undergarments – boys received a loincloth, girls a red underskirt. At the age of 15, his education complete, a boy of the military class had his head shaved in the samurai style and received, as well as his two swords and a man's hat, his adult name. At 16, a girl was presented with her first full-sized *obi*. Both could then take their place in society.

◀ Girls of three and five years old take part in *shichi-go-san*, the festival of the ages.

▲ A five-year-old boy wears a man's trousers for the first time to visit his local shrine. He is playing with a windsock shaped like carp, a symbol of courage.

▼ A doll representing a child performing the dragon dance.

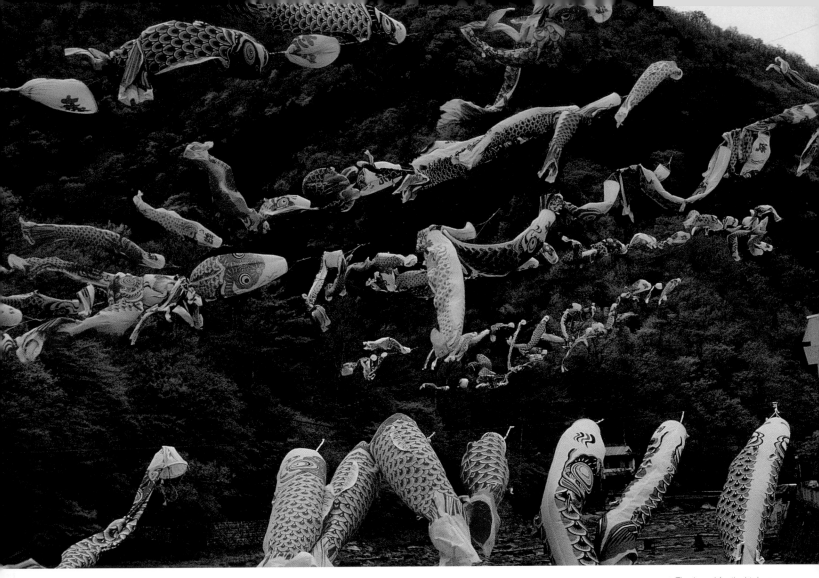

'Rustle in the breeze with all your strength, you young bamboo stems, in the fleeting instant.' Kobayashi Issa (1763–1827).

The martial way

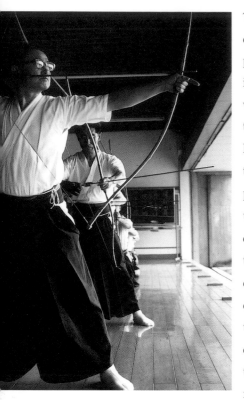

▲ The 'way of the bow', *kyudo*, is one of the active forms of meditation in Zen Buddhism. Based on maintaining an upright posture, it is practised above all as a mental discipline that strives for harmony between man, universe and target.

▶ *Iai-do*, the art of unsheathing a sword, has 20 *kata*, or movements, for drawing the sword and 50 more for cutting with it.

The oldest martial art is sumo, the traditional Japanese style of wrestling which pits two opponents of impressive proportions, wearing special loincloths, against each other in a circular ring that symbolises the heavens. The bout, which is extremely short, is based on concentration, penetration of an opponent's soul and the use of 48 authorised holds. The winner is the wrestler who throws his opponent to the floor or forces him out of the ring. The contest is preceded by a Shinto ritual of exorcism and purification using salt. The other forms of combat were originally a collection of techniques known as 'the way of the bow and the horse' which, from the 13th century, became the 'way of the arts of war', and were used to complete the education of samurai, especially during the Edo period. Initially, at a time when Japan was at peace, they were techniques of defence and attack, then gradually they combined physical training with moral discipline. From this time the term *do*, meaning spiritual 'way', replaced *jutsu*, meaning a martial 'technique'. In 1882 the *jujutsu* of the feudal era became judo, the 'way of suppleness'. The other techniques developed to become *budo*, the 'ways of combat'. From then on physical training, the search for self-control, strength of character, non-violence and respect for an opponent were practised through a series of codes of behaviour and *kata*, stylised forms of action designed to teach the correct movements. These *kata* are also found in unarmed martial arts, such as aikido, judo and karate, as well as in those that use weapons such as kendo, archery, the art of drawing the sword, and that of handling a halberd.

▶ A sumo bout takes place before a large crowd of spectators. The winner is the wrestler who makes his opponent touch the floor in the ring with any part of his body other than his feet, or forces him out of the ring.

Games
and gods

In the past, children's games were regarded as not belonging completely to this world. They were thought to be sparks of the divine, doors opening on to the world of the supernatural. Gradually, however, games left the realm of the transcendental to become an amusement; yet, even today, when children are observed at play, people's memories rediscover that original innocence touched by the sacred. When men ceased to be in contact with their gods, they invented new games based exclusively on human skill and, from the Heian period onwards, people took part in poetry contests, competitions involving incense and games using shells, dice and cards. The Japanese still have a taste for games of chance – as a way of renewing contact with the gods – oracles and games of numbers. Like a religious trance, a game allows someone to be 'transported' elsewhere by intense concentration or the elation of victory. On the other hand, it can also lead to an individual turning in on themselves, as in the case of *pachinko*, Japan's version of billiards, or horse racing. Human beings can thus either be blessed by the gods or possessed by them. In this way, the Japanese passion for nature can be compared to a form of madness. Each year the 'contemplation of the flowers' is taken so seriously that the 'flower-mad' think nothing of travelling from the south of Japan to the north to follow the flowering of the cherry blossom. This kind of aesthetic derangement is nevertheless a way of communicating with nature and thus with the gods. In former times, traditional sports offered a real opportunity to honour the divinities and often to predict the future. This ritual still survives in sumo, although today victory is no longer the work of the gods, but a result of the fighter's prowess.

▲ A musician plays the *shakuhachi*, a long flute whose sound evokes the murmuring of the gods in the bamboo forests.

▼ Every year at the beginning of April, when the cherry trees are in full blossom, Japanese families picnic and groups of friends drink under the trees laden with flowers.

▶ A little girl in a kimono plays with an origami of a crane.

Monkey dances and others

▲ The palanquin makes its appearance at the Hachioji festival. The gods love festivals, especially the comic dances of 'monkeys' and fools.

▼ The festival of souls in Kumamoto is the excuse for an enormous procession in which each district of the city is represented. Participants vie with each other in their high spirits, music, singing and *bon-odori* dancing.

▶ *Buyo* dancing can be seen as a kind of martial art, in which the performer concentrates intensely and each movement has the rigorousness of a *kata*.

Originally, dance was closely connected to religion. The oldest dances re-enacted episodes in the lives of the gods – especially the dance of the goddess Uzume, who coaxed the sun goddess out of her retreat. Masked actors would mime these stories, accompanied by an orchestra of flutes and drums. Buddhism also offered dances of invocation, but the vast majority of dances were folk celebrations that drew on the magical-religious manifestations of pantomime, 'monkey dances', comic interludes, sorcerers' exorcisms, propitiatory rites, jugglers' acts and village processions. As the centuries went by, Japanese dance lost its religious character, but it retained a kind of spiritual quality. From the 16th to the 18th centuries it was gradually codified and evolved towards abstraction, becoming known as *buyo*. Two strands established themselves: *odori* was developed within *kabuki* theatre to express human feelings strongly, and *mai* was more strongly influenced by *no* theatre. The latter, especially widespread in western Japan, flourished chiefly in court circles. There was no concept of virtuosity in these dances: they were performed for their own sake, conveying the physical energy and mental concentration of the dancer, not their vanity. The *miyako odori*, the famous cherry-tree dances performed in spring by *maiko* and geisha, were directly inspired by the 'Kyoto dances', which expressed the elegance and refinement of the Imperial Court. The stylised and demanding movements of *buyo* are slow and full of tension, and still convey the codes of the past, achieving a sort of perfection in the way they recall an event or describe a character.

The performing body

Four types of classical theatre exist side by side in Japan, each answering the deepest needs of the classes that created or encouraged it. *Bugaku* is the essence of aristocratic refinement, while *no*, which had the support of the warrior class, describes the torments of the souls of the past. *Bunraku*, which uses only puppets and *kabuki* are both popular forms of drama, favoured by people who live in big cities for their expression of the moving or cruel beauty of states of mind. While *bugaku*, which was imported from Tang-dynasty China in the 8th century, combines continental choreography with 'elegant music', *no*, *bunraku* and *kabuki* are descended from ancient religious dances called *kagura*, Buddhist rituals and village farces. At once sacred and profane, these forms of drama combine games, dance, singing and music. They also use masks – wooden masks in *no*, puppets in *bunraku*, make-up in *kabuki* – and all sublimate reality to attain an ideal.

No appeared at the end of the 14th century, at a time of great change in Japan. The shogunate of the time, anxious to assert itself in the eyes of the courtiers, encouraged this type of theatre to become a magnificent art form, a sort of spellbinding celebration in dancing and song that could rival the entertainments of the Imperial Court. Its favourite themes – sung in the archaic language of the time, which presents a real test of breathing and voice – are mostly inspired by Buddhism and dwell on the transitory nature of existence. A *no* play lasts about an hour and consists of five or six consecutive pieces. They are so concentrated, however, that they are interspersed with short comic interludes called *kyogen*. In *no* plays, the main character, the *shite*, wears a mask and often represents a supernatural being or the spirit of a hero, a woman or a courtier. The second most important part is played by the *waki*, who may, in exceptional circumstances, wear a mask if playing a female role. The role of the *waki* is to transport the audience to the time and place of the piece's action, and then to make the *shite* reveal the real nature of his or her agonised soul, 'at the crossroads of dreams'. The other characters live in the present and do not wear a mask, but their exposed faces must never show any sign of emotion or change their expressions. The mask is therefore inseparable from *no*. It gives form to a divinity and expresses its power, and of necessity becomes a sacred object, immutable in form. For this reason, actors meditate before they put the mask over their faces. Whether it represents a god, animal, man, woman, ghost or demon, each mask aims to portray a type rather than

The kimono worn by the *onnagata* is loose because it is designed for dancing.

153

an individual. When the craftsman makes it, he does not try to convey a given feeling but rather to sculpt 'the middle expression', an equivocal look close to neutrality. Wearing this undefined face, the *shite* can display the whole range of his talent, conveying the complex internal nuances of his role simply by a tilt of the head or a play of light and shade. The mask then fits with the actor's language of gestures, minutely deconstructed into distinct movements, to express the controlled violence of intense emotions which leads to *yugen*, the intangible 'subtle grace' that goes beyond all common notions of time and space. Dispensing with scenery, apart from a huge pine tree adorning the background of a stage open on three sides, *no* also does without props, except perhaps a fan, a weapon or some highly abstract structure. However, this scenic space, surmounted by a roof resembling that of a Shinto temple, includes a platform for the musicians and extends into a 'bridge' that leads to the foyer, a symbol of the way from this world to the next. It is entirely devoted to conveying the *ma*, the interval between two movements, between the entry and revelation of the *shite*, between the characters and the choir, the dance and the musicians, and dream and reality.

In contrast to the stillness of *no* theatre, charged with deep motives and subtle meanings, *kabuki* is a world of demonstrative gestures and virtuosity. The word *ka-bu-ki* ('music, dance, narrative') supposedly comes from *kabuku*, meaning 'to dress and behave extravagantly'. *Kabuki* was developed later than *no*, and was exclusively for the entertainment of the urban masses. It drew its repertoire from current events in large cities, not from the legendary circles of the old Imperial Court. The people no longer dreamed of ghostly spirits or a warrior's sacrifice, but were challenging and mocking the ruling class, preferring to weep at the impossible loves of a geisha and a rogue. From its beginnings in the 17th century, *kabuki* made great play of the expression of feelings, and reinvented femininity by using men to play female roles. The face was no longer an enigmatic wooden mask but an expressive form of make-up called *kumadori*, as worn by the *onnagata* and *aragoto*, the 'rough' style of hero, one distinguished by delicate white make-up, the other by angry red lines representing veins swollen with blood. In *kabuki*, the theatrical education of the 'ball children' begins at the age of five or six. These child actors learn dancing, acrobatics and the ritual of the tea ceremony. Every day they practise *kata*, apparently fixed models of dramatic techniques and stereotyped actions, to become 'young star actors' and eventually 'idols'. The actors' rigorous training in dance, to achieve control of the body and breathing, in singing to learn pitch and how to distort the voice, and in *shamisen* to educate the ear, allows them, as adults, to command an immense repertoire built up over decades, whose language of gesture they have absorbed until it is second nature. Since dialogue is only secondary in *kabuki*, there is no need to follow the plot to the end, not only because a play lasts for twelve hours or so but because the plot only matters insofar as it leads up to 'big scenes' in which the lead actor displays his talent and charm. Whichever character is being portrayed, he is always in communication with another world, thus becoming a medium, a shaman, or a monk celebrating a rite.

At the beginning of the 20th century, the actor Kawakami Otojiro and the actress Sada Yakko, the first woman to play alongside male actors, tried to modernise Japanese theatre by staging shorter plays, similar to those in Europe, but essentially Japanese in spirit. These lay at the origin of modern Japanese drama – a sort of combination of *kabuki* and the Western-style theatre of ideas, which became extremely significant in the 1950s. The dissident drama of the early 1970s was produced by small companies originating in universities and preoccupied by marginalisation, such as that of Suzuki Tadashi, from Waseda University, imbued with the incantatory drama of Antonin Artaud. But the most astonishing form of underground drama is *buto*, a sort of anti-dance invented in the 1960s by avant-garde artists who wished to express the difficulty of living in a Japan obsessed by the shame of defeat, and who rejected the frenzied materialism of post-war society. Its originator, Hijikata Tatsumi, described it as *ankoku buto* ('dance of darkness'). The other great founder of *buto* was Ono Kazuo, who at the age of almost 80 became famous for playing a celebrated flamenco dancer of the 1920s. At that time, a number of *buto* dancers came from the provinces and asserted a certain rural character which they associated with the 'reverse side' of Japan, the 'real' Japan. In a way, their 'happenings' aimed at a return to the ancient roots of primitive dances, to rediscover the original meaning of Japanese drama. Tanaka Min, one of the great present-day *buto* dancers, who is strongly influenced by the *kagura* of former times, uses his body as a medium, freed from gravity, in order to reintegrate it and imbue it with a 'dancing soul'. In his view, 'dancing reality' was not capable of conveying human experience on its own. For this reason he uses silence and nudity to reveal the vibrations of the body and 'nature and freedom on both sides of the skin'.

'It is the very essence of Japanese entertainment: it requires actors to remain still when they move, that gestures made visible relate to an inner immobility, and that the absence of gesture indicates inner turmoil.'
Ichikawa Ennosuke III.

Acting with the body

Kabuki is a theatre of actors. The audience does not come to follow a plot, but to admire the fascination the actor exerts. The public are always eager for novelty, and expect their idol to bring a fresh interpretation to a role, while still preserving tradition. *Kabuki* thus consists of a series of *coups de théâtre*, physical action and forceful declamations sung in a falsetto voice honed by long training. The notion of *mie*, designed to focus attention on the actor and demonstrate his virtuosity, is often felt as soon as he embarks on the 'way of flowers' that leads to the stage. This sudden entry, backed up by music, is an eagerly awaited moment which, as the actor pauses to be admired, draws cries of encouragement from fans. According to the great actor Ichikawa Ennosuke III, *kabuki* is 'a kind of drama experienced via the body' – not only because of the testing, intense rehearsals, the long hours on stage, the acrobatics, entries and exits and various heroics, but also because of the sudden about-faces, moments of truth in which the actor reveals his character's true nature. Ennosuke remains an unrivalled specialist in sudden changes of costume, which demand considerable energy – because of the combined weight of the many costumes worn one over the other, which are gradually shed in the course of his various metamorphoses – and unflinching physical and mental toughness. This is especially the case when, as in the play *Hitoritabi Gojusan-tsugi*, he plays 18 different parts (seven of them women) and even performs a *chunori* – a flight over the auditorium. To thrill the audience, a virtuous woman may become a monster, a tattooed man in disguise or a heron, and an ordinary man may be transformed into a hero. When a mask comes off, it often reveals another beneath it.

▲ A *kabuki onnagata* in the 1920s.

◄ The *kabuki* actor Ichikawa Ennosuke III, playing the fox Genkuro in the play *Yoshitsune Sembonzakura*, performs a *chunori* over the auditorium.

►► In the *kabuki* play *Yamato Takeru*, the hero scythes the grass in a blazing field where he has been trapped by his enemies. The flames are represented by acrobat-actors.

More feminine
than women

Formerly, when theatre consisted only of dancing, women took an active part in it. For example, the young *shirabyoshi* who, in the late Heian period, praised the warlike feats of the gallant Yoshitsune. The same was true of the female shamans and young professional dancers who officiated at shrines. One of these, the dancer O Kuni, attached to the Izumo shrine, achieved fame in 1603 when, during a tour of Kyoto where she gave some innovative performances combining Buddhist invocations with folk dances, she came on stage sporting baggy, Portuguese-style trousers. These strange dances inspired the crowds and set a trend that spread throughout the country, becoming known as *kabuki odori*. Many female troupes were formed at the start of the Edo period, but since prostitution developed with them, female roles were played by men from 1629, the year women were barred from the stage for encouraging licentiousness. When the young pubescent boys who replaced them also proved an encouragement to prostitution, female roles were given to older men, known as *onnagata*. This role, which became an essential part of the structure of *kabuki*, demanded a permanent transformation in the behaviour of an actor, who was not allowed to copy women. The woman portrayed was never exaggerated, as this would amount to caricature, but properly acted – that is, recreated – to appear totally plausible. During the 19th century, famous *onnagata* made headlines by living as women even off-stage, in order to perfect their parts. So exemplary were their feminine manners and bearing that, in a society with a certain taste for decadence, these were assiduously copied by real women. In *no* plays, the austere nature of the repertoire and the Confucian spirit of the time

▶ Two *onnagata* bow to each other in the *kabuki* play *Yoshitsune Sembonzakura*.

▼ A *bunraku* narrator. Women have only recently been admitted to this traditional form of drama, formerly reserved for men.

relegated women to a lower rank: they were considered incapable of conveying the soul of a warrior at the Imperial Court and femininity appeared on stage only in the unreal form of a mask. Today, classical theatre is still seen as men's work. The stage is still forbidden to the so-called weaker sex and women's parts are played by male actors. These are all the harder to play because *kabuki* presents a multitude of subtleties and varieties of female behaviour. Rather than simply interpreting a woman's part, the actor 'is' a woman, with shoulders held low, feet turned inwards, undulating neck, graceful movements of the hands and sleeves, body bent forward, a humble and submissive attitude, and a thin voice – characteristics that a male actor would naturally reject in everyday life. The *bunraku* puppet theatre is also a men's theatre. Until recently the puppets were only manoeuvred by men and it is only latterly that women have been able to act as narrators or play the *shamisen*. In a wider context, women have only very recently been allowed backstage to prepare costumes and make-up, but there is still a strong reluctance to accept them as members of choirs or groups of musicians. Apart from the 'new *kabuki* theatre' in Osaka, which allows women in its productions, the only truly feminine classical theatre is in the dances performed by geisha and *maiko*, who give annual displays of their acting talents. Then, as if to take their revenge on society, they play male roles. They do not idealise them, however, but only copy them in order to mock them.

The smile
of the mask

▲ A *bugaku* mask with a mobile chin-piece, used in dances from the 'left side', which represents China.

▶ A *no* mask of a young woman.

In *no* theatre, the mask most laden with meaning is that of the young woman. It symbolises Japanese theatre by itself. Because it is completely ambiguous, it is seen as its most faithful expression. In fact, it represents the mask of a spirit from beyond the grave that fleetingly takes the form of a princess with a hint of a smile. The smooth white face, with its neutral expression, can express a wide range of emotions according to the lighting and the actor's ability. The mask's smile, motionless and filled with purpose, can then be used to convey an innocent lightness, guileful seductiveness, devouring passion or pain. Sometimes, however, the part demands that several masks be worn in succession, especially for conveying the demonic frenzy of someone who has gone from the enigmatic calm of a woman of the court to the fiendish behaviour of an adulteress, with her pointed horns and carnivore's teeth. Like the make-up in *kabuki*, the mask used in *no* is 'woman' rather than representing a specific woman. It makes use only of the essentials: the eyes for seeing and the mouth for expressing itself. This idea of hiding the reality of the human face in order to portray the beauty of the soul goes back to ancient times, when the delicate ladies of the Heian court already looked like insubstantial representations of women. The design of the mask, framed by the ordered, dark border of painted hair, reflects the person's inner experience more faithfully than the real face of a princess set in her time and place. It is an attempt to gather together all human expressions – aggression, bitterness, pleasure, kindness and tenderness – in the purity of a single smile, that of a woman. The ambiguous smile of the *no* woman is therefore connected to the idea of sin and redemption in Zen. It is the final state of all Japanese smiles.

Dance of darkness

Buto dance takes its name from *bu*, 'to dance', and *to*, 'to trample underfoot' It is a form of return to remote sources such as the Shinto dances, pantomimes, Buddhist invocations, exorcisms and shamanistic trances of ancient Japan. As then, *buto* uses grotesque bodily and facial contortions; the dancers often seem anchored to the ground, or to mud or asphalt, rejecting the soaring movements of Western dance and the refined aesthetic of *buyo*. 'Moving the upper parts of the body calms the spirit, moving the feet stimulates it,' says the dancer Murobushi Ko, stressing that *buto* dance 'does not lead to a trance or look to the future' but opens the eyes to what is always there, the intimate relationship between the body and nature, born of the primeval chaos. Like other dramatic forms, *buto* demands a profound sense of bodily discipline. One idea it contains is that of rediscovering the meaning of movement through situations of extreme tension – slow convulsions, exasperating immobility and sudden spasms – to allow the body, seen as a chrysalis, to free the human being and celebrate its unity with the universe, beyond good and evil and beyond the disorder of life. As in traditional drama, body make-up, usually covering the entire body, constantly replays its classic role of creating absence, masking the actor with white so that his body, freed from its habitual limits, can become an object that is part of the world. Often this body is naked, but some productions require costumes – magnificent rags or ashen clothes – to allow the tortured gestures to seem more like meditations, to eradicate the trauma of Hiroshima and give utterance to destruction, life, death, dreams and the sacred.

▲ The *buto* dancer Tanaka Min, his body covered with ashes.

◀ The *buto* dancer Carlotta Ikeda.

▶▶ The *buto* dancer Carlotta Ikeda.

▶▶ *Buto* dancers often convey their message via naked bodies completely covered by make-up, but sometimes highly sophisticated costumes are designed in order to go beyond the body

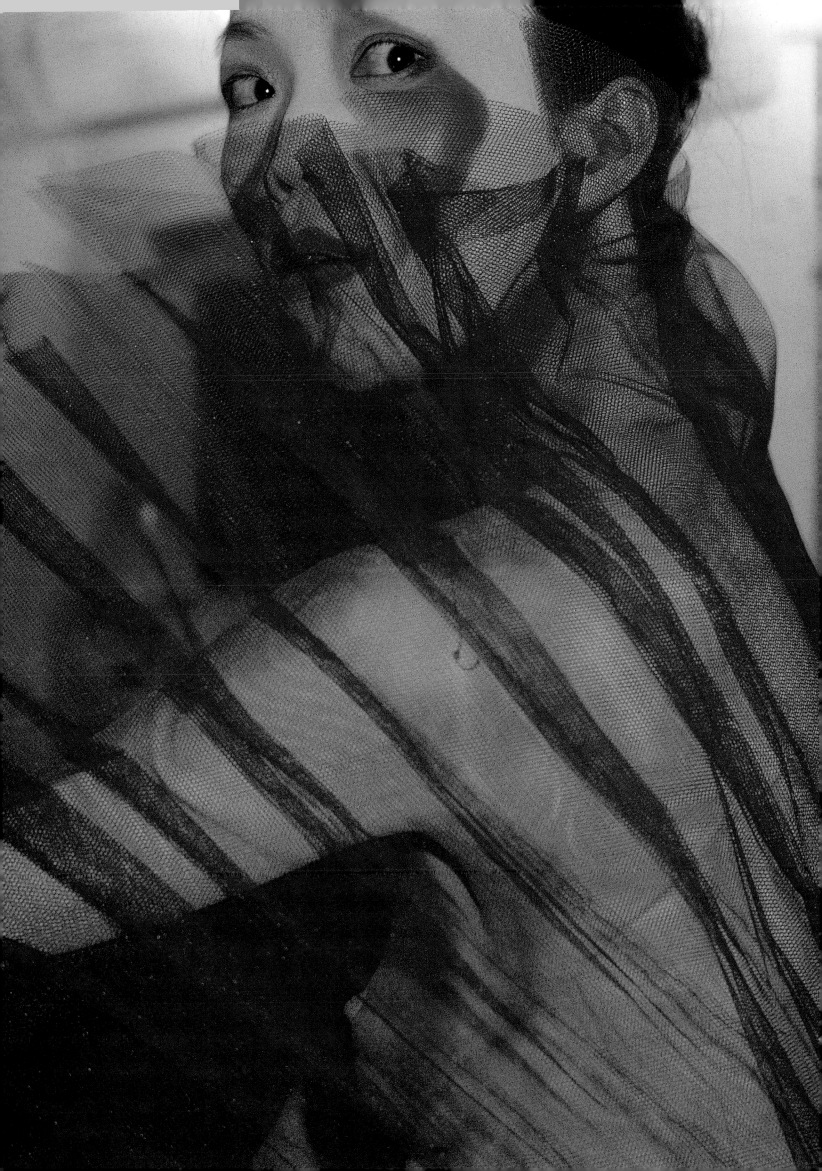

Extravagant costumes

▲ Shunjo, *The Actor Ichikawa Danjuro in the Costume of Shibaraku*, about 1787. Janette Ostier Collection, Paris.

▼ *Kabuki* costume to be worn by a powerful character.

▶ The *kabuki* actor Ichikawa Ennosuke III adjusts the wig of the lion-father in the play *Renjishi*. The climax of the drama is a dance performed by two lions, father and son.

In Japanese drama, well-informed audiences are especially keen on the beauty of the costumes and the way the actor gets the best out of them throughout the play. Measured steps, reticent gestures, a quickened pace, falls and surprises bring to life the kimonos whose shapes and colours all carry symbolic and narrative meanings. In *no*, costume provides visual support and is an aesthetic extension of the mask, made sacred by the actor's art. The mask is slightly smaller than a human face and makes the body look slightly longer than it is. It also helps to magnify the costume which, with its gold and silver cloth subtly catching the light, makes the characters appear all the more supernatural. The actor's vulnerable body disappears altogether, giving way to a ghostly body conveyed by the tightly woven costume, which is starched to stiffen its outlines. This accentuates the dance steps, rendering them more geometric and making them appear slower. In contrast, *kabuki* theatre aims to externalise feelings and uses extravagant costumes with designs and accessories that contribute to the understanding of the character. However, the astonishing shapes of some costumes demand a special language of gesture. For example, mythical warriors carry an enormous knot of rope on their backs which limits their arm movements to rotating only in the same plane as the body. Some costumes bearing specific decorative motifs – such as a combination of waves and demons – can only be worn by specially trained actors because they demand intensive mental preparation. The kimono worn by an *onnagata*, especially that of the courtesan, is a woman's garment specially designed to fit a man's body. These costumes are usually heavy and require physical strength on the part of the wearer, which is gradually acquired through regular dance practice.

The shadow
of the dolls

Popular Japanese theatre makes use of a stagehand known as the 'shadow'. In *kabuki* this helper, dressed and hooded in black, is meant to be invisible to the audience. Like a shadow, he never leaves the actor, passing him any props he needs and acting as his dresser and prompter. At one time his tasks even included holding a candle up to the actor's face so that the audience did not miss the slightest detail of his facial movements during *mie*. The 'shadow' is still used in *bunraku* puppet theatre, though here he is no longer a stagehand but a puppetmaster. More than just a handler, this ghostly figure dressed in dark robes is really an actor. His whole body is used to convey expression, movement and feelings. His gestures exactly parallel those of the puppet, but he humbly effaces himself before the eternal nature of the protagonist, a figure of carved wood. At the beginning of the 17th century, puppets were quite small and had no legs, and each was controlled by one handler. Gradually, these figures acquired mechanisms for moving the eyes, opening the mouth, frowning and moving the joints of the hands. Soon they needed three handlers to operate one puppet, each with a precise job according to their experience. The chief handler is the one who really gives the puppet life. His left hand carries the puppet from inside the body, turns its head and works the keys that operate the mobile parts of the face, while his right hand operates the puppet's right arm. The first assistant moves the left arm and the second assistant works the legs. The whole effect of *bunraku* depends on the three 'shadows' working in perfect harmony and co-ordinating their movements with the wailing of the *shamisen* musical accompaniment and the cries of the narrator.

◀ A *bunraku* puppet from Awaji representing the child O-Tsuru in the play *Keisei Awa Naruto*. It is operated by three masked handlers.

▼ A 'shadow' in ceremonial costume adjusts the *obi* of the *kabuki onnagata* Sawamura Tojuro, who is playing a princess.

空間
Spatial relationships

All bodies necessarily occupy a space, but in some countries this obvious fact acquires a cultural dimension. In Japan, the body occupies a place that relates particularly to a strictly physical space – as defined by architecture or the language of gestures – but it is also totally subject to a much more subtle space: its relationship with the sacred. The first space in which the body is involved is that of nature. Whereas Westerners influence nature to shape it to their wishes, often creating a world governed more by their thoughts than by their sensitivities, the Japanese prefer to see mankind as subjugated by the cosmos, and so obliged to melt, curl up and integrate itself into space without seeking to dominate it. As a small link in a complex, infinite chain, they believe that fundamentally they owe more to nature than to society and that when they alter nature – as in a garden or a *bonsai* tree – they do this to make it comprehensible at all times and to remind themselves that they owe it everything. The Japanese do not have an anthropomorphic view of nature: on the contrary, they see it in its tiniest details, perceiving the world intuitively through all the senses and deriving pleasure from its irregularities and asymmetries. For this reason, a Japanese is usually indifferent to the high seas, great mountains and endless plains – to any landscape without limits upon it. He is used to living in landscapes on the scale of a garden, whose background is always reassuring – Mount Fuji, the outline of a hill, a forest of Japanese cedar or pine, a screen of bamboo. These horizons, seen from the veranda, are tirelessly celebrated in poetry and painting. But in reality the Japanese love these natural elements not for their external beauty, but for the way they suggest mental images; they have a feeling for the poetry of fleeting instants and love to meditate on the atmosphere of springs, rocks and trees. As a Shinto proverb makes clear: 'The man who is in harmony with nature can only do good.'

In the Japanese house, the body itself is the key to the space it builds around it. In the Japanese mind – which thinks in terms of units of surface and volume, not in a linear fashion as in the West – the area occupied by a man lying down determines the dimensions of the *tatami*, the straw mat that is an element in architecture and conditions all behaviour within the house. Removing shoes before entering a room, kneeling down to open a door, holding a conversation, admiring the garden, lying down to sleep – all these are everyday actions that make the house a living space on a human scale. Apart from the kitchen and bathroom, space in Japanese architecture

The *tokonoma* of a feudal house in the Niigata district. The *tokonoma* is considered a sacred space on certain occasions, and governs the position and behaviour of the people near it.

is moveable. Rooms with *tatami* are empty places without a specific function and equipped with sliding partitions, which become temporarily functional at bedtime, at mealtimes, during games or when receiving guests. Only one space can be considered to have a specific function: the *tokonoma*, a small alcove sunk into a wall adjacent to the garden, which contains a painting, an objet d'art, or a flower arrangement. The room that contains it is used to receive honoured guests and, when a meal is served, the most important person is seated in front of it. This fluidity of space, using the interplay of removable sliding screens, means that no specialised piece of furniture is a fixture; folding tables and futons are stored away in cupboards built into the partitions. Modern urban houses, with their small fixed rooms, no longer allow this flexible use of space and need to be organised on the basis of specific functions. Aside from the sober character of its spaces, the Japanese house is notable for the sensual quality of the materials used in its construction and for the interplay of light and shade. Light filtered through paper windows, the discreet colours of wood, straw and paper and the palpable vibrations of the areas in shadow favour peace and give meaning to emptiness. Houses are the realm of fine aromas and rare fragrances, filled with the scents of the straw in the *tatami*, certain woods, incense in the *butsudan*, sandalwood in the kimono chests, and scents from the garden. Although a house may be furnished only with shade and filtered light, noises muffled by straw and paper conspire to produce inner silence and melancholy – pierced in summer by the ceaseless song of the cicada and the cawing of crows.

Living on floors covered with *tatami* requires special ways of sitting, sleeping, eating, working and dreaming. People never dominate space: they see it in their peripheral vision and only rarely vertically, as they do with the *tokonoma* alcove. This relationship with architecture is connected to a particular body shape which has a low centre of gravity, very muscular legs and a long trunk. The politest way to sit is kneeling, the feet stretched out backwards with one resting lightly on the other, buttocks on heels and hands on thighs. Since the blood has difficulty circulating in the lower foot, the feet may be reversed from time to time. After a long period spent in this constricting position, a more flexible seated position is allowed in which the legs are positioned slightly to the side, so that the feet no longer bear the body's entire weight. A woman dressed in Western clothing can also adopt this more relaxed position, while a man wearing trousers can simply sit cross-legged. Living at floor level has also produced a whole set of rules. For example, to open a sliding screen a person must kneel at an oblique angle to it, place the hand farther away from it on the *tatami*, put the other hand into a small decorative notch cut into the panel and gently open it with a sideways movement. Once the screen is partly open, the hand must be lowered a few centimetres before opening it completely. The same procedure applies to closing it. Lying down on a *tatami* mat is much simpler: all that is required is to pull the futon out of its closet and spread it on the floor in such a way that the sleeper's head is towards the *tokonoma*.

The house is also the realm of draughts of air. Nothing is designed to be airtight, but is actually meant to have air blowing through it. For this reason, the main rooms face south, so that they are sheltered from the north wind in winter and enjoy the breeze that always blows from the south in summer. Winter is never bitter in most of the islands of

Japan, so houses, like kimonos, are designed principally to ease the discomfort of the hot, humid summer. The aim is to catch the cooler air at floor level on the veranda and over the *tatami*, where people sit, so that it enters the sleeves and keeps the neck cool. The pleasures of Japanese life include many visual, olfactory and culinary elements designed to make unpleasant weather more bearable. For example, before modern technology was used to combat heat, the Japanese had devised other, more subtle means to suggest visually the cool of dawn or of a stream. To this end, they chose porcelain crockery with blue motifs recalling whirlwinds or waves; receptacles in tinted, blown or frosted glass reminiscent of a light early-morning mist; wood whose lacquer shone like droplets of water, and chopsticks in green bamboo. On the veranda, they shivered when they heard the sharp tinkle of the *furin* bell hanging from the porch roof. In his relationship with space, mankind comes face to face with certain concepts concerning the nature of time and place; equally, he is subject to the notion of sacred space. The rhythm of life is defined by the concepts of *hare* and *ke*. *Hare* refers to special times, recognised by society and made sacred, such as birth, starting school, promotion at work and marriage. *Ke* describes the process of passing from one to another of these exceptional situations. Ideally, these interludes should be calm and peaceful, for the natural rhythm of human life demands a serene alternation between the secular and the sacred. Thus the New Year is *hare*, as are festivals or other occasions when ancestors are honoured. Certain places can also be described as sacred or secular. In the home there are certain permanent sacred spaces such as Shinto and Buddhist domestic altars, but other places only become sacred temporarily, for example during a ceremony – for instance, the *tokonoma* in the principal room, or the area bounded by the golden screen unfolded for a wedding.

House
and kimono

Thanks to the *tatami*, the Japanese grow up accustomed to living at floor level and their dress has been designed for kneeling on the floor. The kimono is a simple strip of material about 12 m (39 ft) long and 33 to 38 cm (13 to 15 in) wide, cut into seven straight sections which are stitched edge to edge. Like the *tatami*, it is standardised and universal. Like the house, which changes constantly according to the use being made of it, the kimono effortlessly adapts to all body shapes; it can be worn from childhood to adulthood without needing complex alterations. The kimono is closely linked to architecture, not only because the latter obliges people to live at floor level, but also because of the harmony of the materials used to make it. The wood, straw, paper and bamboo of the house combine with the silk, cotton and hemp of garments to form a link between house-nature and body-universe. The kimono also matches the seasons and the landscape; its designs always show a restricted vision of space, such as might be seen from a veranda. This sober harmony between person, house, dress and nature is always tinged with a certain kind of melancholy, solitude and inner silence. For the Japanese, the kimono is *the* essential gar-ment: refined over the centuries, it is also a subtle reflection of life and marks the passage of time – the seasons, stages in a person's life and the generations. It is the ephemeral symbol of beauty, love, regret, and also of the significant and less important times of life. Nevertheless, the kimono is ill-suited to modern life, where the odds are against its survival. If young women today are reluctant to wear it, this is not because it is uncomfortable but because they refuse to be abstract images and want to express their body and personality.

◀ Opening a partition in a traditional house involves kneeling down beforehand.

▼ Since indoor space is made up of 'noble' parts such as the *tatami*, where people live, eat and sleep, shoes must be removed before entering. In this way the contamination of the outside world does not penetrate the house.

▶ A house in Takayama, in the Japanese Alps. The areas with wooden floors and those covered in *tatami* are clearly separated from those with a mud floor, which are regarded as belonging to the outside even though they are inside the house.

▶▶ The flexible nature of traditional Japanese rooms means that they can be transformed to suit a given function by the simple addition of removable elements, such as folding tables for meals. Floor areas covered with *tatami* are meant to be knelt on.

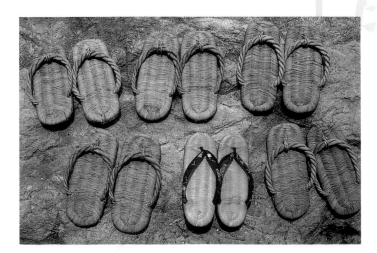

Veranda
and street

The body is closely involved in that conception of Japanese architectural space based on the tension between the edges of two surfaces, called *en*. This intermediate space, far from setting two opposite ideas or places against each other, is the place where one space passes to the other. In traditional architecture, the veranda does not separate the house from the garden: it is neither inside, because it opens out on to the garden, nor outside, because it is sheltered by its roof; it is the synthesis of both spaces. A person sitting on the veranda is at the heart of this ambiguity, which allows nature to enter the house and the house to be open to the world. The traditional street has the same character: the opposition between private and public is barely perceived there. It is similar to a corridor, but one that is outside the house. Residents wash it down with water every morning, children play there and shopkeepers put out their stalls and people relax there in the evening, often wearing the *yukata*, the kimono worn after a bath. Outside life can be seen from within the house, but it stops at the front door, beyond which is the realm of the private; to underline this fact and to keep the *tatami* free of impurities from outside, shoes must be removed before entering. For this reason, a guest cannot come in without first having bowed at a distance of several paces and apologised for imposing his or her presence. Japanese people also love to plunge into the life of the city; they enjoy the crowds strolling about in the shopping areas and cannot resist the noisy passion of stadiums and places of entertainment. They would be lost without the loud exhortations of advertising, without the advice hammered out all day long in department stores, in trains and at traffic lights, and without the lights and neon signs of the city.

▲ In the working-class areas of cities, many of the small restaurants are only separated from the street by a *noren*, a cotton door-curtain which acts as a sign and marks the boundary of an indeterminate area between the outside and the interior.

▼ When a visitor is welcomed or leaves, there are formal greetings which vary according to the guest's importance. The distance between the hosts and the guest indicates the degree of gratitude existing between them.

◄ Ever since the 16th century, tea houses have had low entrances which could not be passed through without bending the back. This 'door of humility' was originally designed to prevent warriors entering the tea house with their weapons.

'Mountains and
gardens penetrate even
into the summer chamber.'
Basho (1644–1694)
Poet and Zen monk

▲ The veranda is the place that expresses *en*, the spatial tension between the house and the garden. Far from setting off the house's interior against the exterior, the veranda 'is' the house.

◄ A huge torchlit procession down Mount Fuji marks the end of the season for climbing it, and the departure of the last of the tourists. After this 'closing ceremony' the mountain reverts to being a sacred space, the peaceful dwelling place of the goddess Kono-hana-Sakuya hime.

Space and time

▲ The flat fan used in *matsuri*, thrust into the belt of a summer kimono, indicates the beginning of an intermediate time, between everyday life and participation in a celebration that verges on the sacred.

▶ The *kabuki* actor Ichikawa Ennosuke III adjusts the wig of the lion-father in the play *Renjishi*. The climax of this work is a dance performed by two lions, father and son.

Ma is also a concept of space, but it introduces the idea of time by referring to the 'emptiness' between two objects or events which follow each other. It is widely used in theatre, music, dance and martial arts, and also in painting and literature. In martial arts, it is the distance separating two opponents and the moment when they are at one in the harmony of combat. In music, it is an aesthetic of silence which derives its power from the tension between two sounds. In theatre, as in dance, it could be described as a 'pause' between two movements which, suggesting an infinity of possible intentions, stimulates the spectator's imagination. 'There, neither score nor text can express the silence of a space torn by the lone sound of the flute or shattered by the throbbing of drums, or given rhythm by the serene echo of strings. It is a world of inexpressible emotion.'[10] In *kabuki*, at the height of a scene's dramatic tension, *ma* is marked by the actors adopting exaggerated and sometimes grimacing poses known as *mie* or 'blinding images'. At this moment, in a spasm of stillness, they must act with the greatest subtlety to fulfil all their role's potential for the audience. The latter's attention is then drawn to the clattering of small wooden blocks or by music. The whole of a play hinges on these culminating moments when, through their immobility, the cast become living sculptures which thrill the audience and bring a burst of applause. Costumes must be perfectly ordered at such moments; sometimes, before the *mie*, a stagehand appears and adjusts their folds, revealing the large family coats of arms that celebrated actors wear on their costumes to show that they are descended from a long dynasty of actors.

10. Keiko Ohara,
Esthétique du Japon
[Japanese aesthetics], Paris,
Éditions Jean-Michel Place, 1990.

◀▲ For the Japanese, nature
is the space where a sacred
harmony reigns, kept alive for
centuries by poetry and by the
spectacular changes in the
country's seasons.

◀◀A folding screen decorated
with gold leaf, showing a
woman of the court playing
with her cat. The screen
temporarily marks the
boundaries of spaces and
can be used to define them.

'The couple had gone
out on to the veranda. And there,
before the sky lit by the dawning day,
tasting the morning air fresh as
mint water on each other's lips,
seeking with their tongues in
each other's mouths a
remnant of warmth, a memory
of a night that was dying,
they kissed.'

Mishima Yukio, *Love at dawn*.

Stealing knowledge from the master

▲ For centuries the Japanese love of natural materials has fostered craftsmanship of the highest quality, whose secrets are handed down the generations, as with this potter in Bizen.

▶ Since the sword is considered to be the soul of the samurai, forging it is a religious rite. Only after a long purification process does the blacksmith, dressed like a Shinto priest, begin to hammer the block of metal.

All Japanese arts are closely linked to everyday life, and involve movement in space or rhythm in time. Paintings can be rolled up and unrolled, screens can be unfolded, a kimono only exists if it is worn, lacquers are always functional. The Japanese like to define themselves through ideal objects – coded images that transform the real into something sacred – and to transform gestures into rituals.

A perfect object created by a craftsman flatters the ability of its user to create beauty; and the user, by buying something, acknowledges the great skill of the craftsman. This reciprocity can only happen through the quality of the work – not just its functional quality but above all its 'creative' and aesthetic qualities, and its ability to rouse the emotions; these allow the ritual rules of the transaction to be realised. Objects are therefore cultural symbols, and through their complicity with the object the art lover can appreciate, through their own gestures, those of the craftsman who fashioned it. This quest for quality is not confined to the quality of the object alone but extends to the relationship between the craftsman and the customer. In Japan, it can be said that selling something to someone means accepting a personal relationship with that individual and accepting part of their spiritual essence. The object then becomes an intermediate space, a sort of synthesis between the customer who uses it and the craftsman who makes it – one doing no more than carry out the wishes of the other. Without this ritualised relationship between the maker and user of a traditional object, such objects would soon be relegated to the world of nostalgia and folklore. Japanese creativity is based essentially on techniques being handed down by practical rather than theoretical means. For an apprentice craftsman, joining a workshop is like entering a religious order. The rules are simple: he has to carry out the most thankless and repetitive tasks to acquire an intimate understanding of the materials, while the master has the noble task of working the material. For several years – usually five – the apprentice does nothing more than look after the master's household and well-being. He then spends the next five years getting used to the tools and carrying out menial tasks. In the final five years, as he perfects his skills,

he has to steal his master's knowledge. In reality, a craftsman never teaches his art and is content merely to practise it. The pupil thus has only one option: to practise the techniques of his craft until they become as assured as those of his master. He can then leave him and set up his own workshop, but he remains duty bound to apply his acquired knowledge intact and without changes. Only on his master's death can he finally develop his own art and take the risk of offering his own original creations. A craftsman is an interpreter of nature, and adapts to its whims. In the final analysis, only the material can determine form, which in turn dictates the specific use of an object when it is adapted for humans. In this context, and to make the reference to nature universal, forms must remain modest so as to conceal the craftsman's skill and show only the essence of an object.

The closer an artisan comes to perfection, the more he must introduce imperfection into his work to render that perfection imaginable. This way of thinking is quite close to Zen Buddhism, as the actions of everyday life become objects of contemplation and meditation. So it is not surprising that many professional tools are worshipped through a particular god, and that the warriors of former times spoke of their sword not as a weapon but as a soul.

▲ A craftsman makes a bamboo basket for a flower arrangement to be used during tea-drinking.

◀ To make travel on foot easier, the Japanese in the Edo period developed a large range of very light folding objects in bamboo and paper, such as umbrellas and lanterns.

the body
in death

In Japan, death is at the centre of life: the souls of the dead are ever-present, living in nature and taking part in everyday life. There is a bond of mutual dependence between the dead and the living, who feel judged, approved of, or condemned by them. Every Buddhist house has a domestic altar where the mortuary tablets of ancestors are kept: it is a place for offerings and prayers, since the dead need to feel the affection of the living for them. In Shinto, souls continue to inhabit their former dwelling places and the houses of their descendants. Having become *kami*, they retain the characters they had in life, whether good or bad, and acquire supernatural powers through death; they have the power to do evil as well as good and are benevolent if offerings are made to them, malevolent if they are neglected. According to Buddhist thinking, ancestors who are worshipped return to earth every year for the festival of *o-bon*. Formerly, workers and apprentices were granted their only holidays in the year at the time of that festival, so that they could join their families and honour their ancestors.

Japanese funerals are highly complex. Specialist organisations are responsible for the rites, be these Shinto or Buddhist, especially with regard to the washing and dressing of the deceased. In a Buddhist funeral, the immediate family and relatives begin by holding a vigil over the recumbent body, which is laid pointing northwards, with the head covered by a piece of white material. Offerings of salt and water are placed near the pillow, together with a bowl of rice with chopsticks projecting from it. Sticks of incense are burned continuously. In former times, coins were also placed near the body to pay for the crossing of the river to the Other World, as well as a knife or sword that symbolically drove away demons. Then the farewell ceremony is held, bringing together the dead person's acquaintances. The monk addresses a few words to the spirit of the deceased so that it may leave the world of *maya* illusions and travel unencumbered to the world of reincarnations, attaining the paradise of the West where the Buddha Amida reigns. As their names are called out, the guests present their condolences and go before the altar to burn incense. 'Money for incense', contained in a special envelope, together with fruit, cakes or a mortuary crown are given to the mourning family. The deceased meanwhile has been placed, according to Buddhist custom, in a crouched position, head against knees, in a narrow coffin of cypress wood which is either cubic or cylindrical in shape. At the end of the service, the coffin is taken to the crematorium and incinerated. The relatives then use chopsticks to

Funerary steles in the form of stupas in a bamboo wood in Kyoto.

gather up a few bones, pass them from person to person and put them in an urn which is placed in the home, next to the deceased's photograph, along with a censer and the funerary tablet bearing their name. The urn is buried in the cemetery 49 days after the cremation. These rites have given rise to a certain number of superstitions. Thus living people must not sleep with their head to the north, cross the right side of their kimono lapel over the left, stick their chopsticks into rice (a symbol of the last meal), or pass food from one pair of chopsticks to another, as is done with the deceased's bones after cremation. All these actions are thought to be inauspicious and capable of attracting death. In Shinto funerals, the body is laid out in a coffin, as in the West, and placed before the altar beside a table made of unpainted wood bearing lit candles and vases of flowers. The priest purifies all those present, then bows before the coffin, lays offerings of food and drink on the altar, recites a lamentation and prays for the deceased. The closest relatives then read out messages of condolence and each guest goes before the altar, bowing and placing a twig from a *sakaki*, the sacred tree of Shinto, on the funerary table according to a strict ritual.

In the past, there were three codes governing mourning: for priests, for the nobility and for warriors. Only the last has survived, in very conservative families. Mourning consisted chiefly of wearing clothes suited to the circumstances, refraining from eating all meat for between three and 50 days, and visiting the deceased's grave at precise times. The duration of mourning also depended on the closeness of a relative, ranging from seven days for first cousins to 13 months for natural or adoptive parents. A husband also demanded 13 months' mourning, but a wife or eldest son warranted only 90 days. No mourning clothes were worn for children younger than three months: only the *bodhisattva* Jizo, residing at the frontier between the real world and that of the dead, could rescue them and feel compassion for them. For children younger than seven, rites differed from those for adults. Today the rules are much less strict than they once were: mourning ends on the 35th or 49th day among Buddhists and on the 50th day for Shintoists. When a person dies, their relatives are impure and for a certain period must not visit a shrine or take part in a celebration or festival. To mark the end of mourning the family gives a *kiake*, an appropriate but inexpensive gift, to each person who made an offering to the spirit of the deceased and to those who helped with the funeral.

Death in Japan also involves some surprising customs, some of which astonished foreign visitors at the beginning of the last century. One of these meant accepting that a person could officially die on a different day from that of their true death. The aim of this custom was usually to bestow on the deceased some further honour and to help the family by paying them a bigger pension. This use of a fictitious date was widely practised during the Edo period, when the government was trying to establish lords in their fiefdoms and so avoid any risk of rebellion. They were then forbidden to die outside their territories; if they did, their families would be exiled, their property seized and their castles annexed. To get round this, clans would not announce the death of their master until the body had been repatriated. As well as dying on their own land, they also had to be buried there. For this reason, devout Buddhists kept a tomb near the founder of their sect during their lifetime, for example the *shingon* necropolis at

Koya San, where they were buried after their death, while their ashes officially rested in the cemetery on their estate.

The glorification of death is also an old tradition in Japan, especially among warriors, most of whom were destined to become ancestors before reaching old age. This is why it has been said that 'the virtue that gives the Japanese people strength is the way they excel at dying'. Since suicide was not considered a sin, for a long time pride drove people to choose death over a survival that inflicted the ills of old age or shame on other people. In the very distant past some men, known as *hito-bashira* ('human pillars') would agree to be buried alive to secure the goodwill of the gods and ensure that a planned building would last. On the death of an emperor, all his servants were sacrificed – a practice that lasted until the dawn of our era, when Suinin decided that these victims should be replaced by clay effigies. Suicide committed in sympathy – to accompany a lord or a husband in death – became over the centuries a demonstration of absolute devotion, and *seppuku* (wrongly termed *harakiri*), which cleansed the honour of a samurai, became an example to all. During the Edo period, the double suicide of lovers, though forbidden by the government, was also seen as the highest form of romanticism: practised chiefly among courtesans, this *joshi* inspired literature, art and theatre. By contrast, the willing self-sacrifice of old women who, in times of scarcity, would have their sons take them to a mountain hermitage to die, so that there would be one less mouth to feed, was distinctly less theatrical. Such total selflessness was proof that the humblest villager had no reason to envy even the most ferocious warrior. This 'love of death' was also sought, during the last war, to convince thousands of young people known as *kamikaze* ('divine winds'), to die in the flower of their youth for the god Japan.

▶▶ Lanterns at the Yasukuni-jinja shrine in Tokyo. Every year during the *bon*, the paths of this imperial shrine, dedicated to the souls of those who died for their country, are lit by thousands of lanterns placed as offerings by the faithful.

The art of dying

Suicide committed in sympathy was regularly banned throughout Japanese history, but on many occasions samurai or servants would kill themselves to follow their masters into the next world. During the Edo period, voluntary suicide by disembowelment – *seppuku* – even became an art of dying among the warrior class. For a samurai to hang, drown or poison himself was seen as the most cowardly of suicides. Even killing oneself using a firearm was considered an ignoble and base way of shuffling off this mortal coil. Only a woman was allowed to kill herself by means other than *seppuku*; the wedding gifts given to her by her husband included a dagger for cutting her throat should she have a moral obligation to do so. Someone would commit *seppuku* if they felt dishonoured, had suffered a serious defeat or wished to demonstrate their good faith in a dramatic way. The most extraordinary kind was *kanshi*, suicide committed in protest at some injustice. Legal disembowelment to make amends for an 'honourable' wrongdoing was a privilege granted to the samurai so that, even in death, they could remain an example to society. The right way of sitting down on the mat in the space designated for suicide, of bowing to the spectators at the start of the ceremony, undoing the white kimono covering the upper part of the body, attaching its sleeves round the knees so as to fall face forwards, plunging the dagger into the left side, making the incision towards the right without flinching and, finally, making the required signal to the *kaishakunin*, the second, to administer the final decapitation – all these actions were expected to be carried out scrupulously and were part of the instruction all samurai had to receive from the chief of military ceremonies.

► Lanterns at the *mitama matsuri* in Shizuoka during the festival of souls.

▼ General Nogi and his wife, photographed a few hours before they committed suicide to follow the Meiji emperor in death.

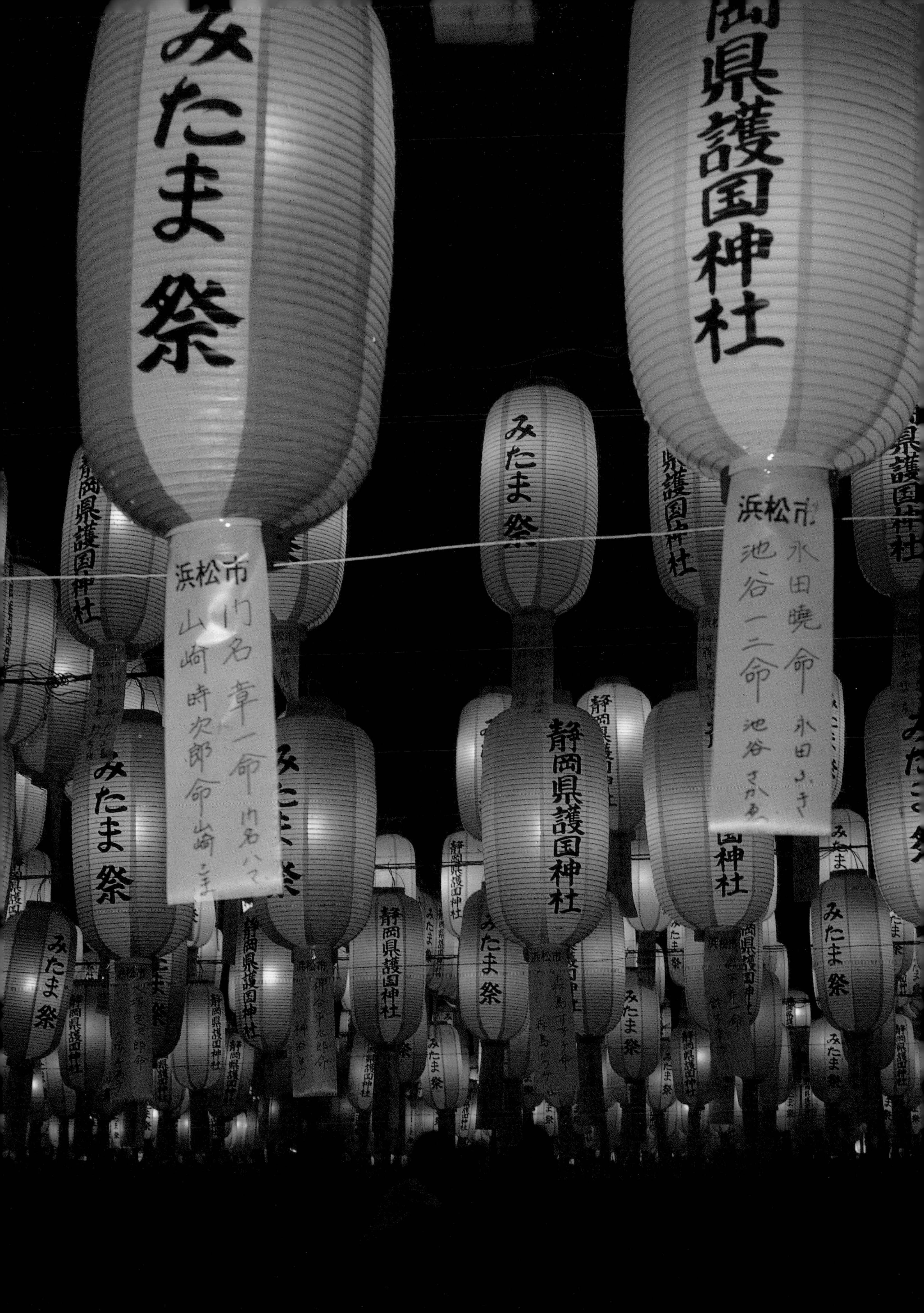
みたま祭
岡県護国神社
浜松市
竹名章一命
山崎時次郎命
浜松市
永田暁命
池谷一二命
静岡県護国神社

Welcoming their ancestors

The word *bon* or *urabon* is the Japanese translation of the Sanskrit word *ulambana*, meaning 'terrible affliction'. This festival of ancestors, which was introduced at the Imperial Court in 657 and became popular in the 10th century, has been celebrated ever since and lasts three days. According to the lunar calendar, 13 July is the day the dead are supposed to return to earth to visit their families. On this first day of the festival, when the spirits descend to the world of the senses, the head of the family solemnly opens the *butsudan*, the domestic altar. Then, followed by the entire family, he visits the cemetery to sprinkle the tomb with water and decorate it with offerings of fruit and vegetables to welcome the souls of the ancestors. A lantern is lit to guide the soul to the house, where it will be accommodated in the *butsudan*, taking up residence in the flame of the candle. When the cemetery is too far from the house, a welcome fire of hemp twigs is lit by the front door to light the way for the soul. On 14 July, the day is devoted to 'renewing acquaintance', sharing meals and introducing new members of the household, while incense burns on the altar. On the last day, a lantern is again lit to accompany the souls back to the spirit world. If the family lives near a river or the sea, the custom is to send them back by placing the lantern on small paper boats that are left to drift on the water. That evening joyful dances, often accompanied by libations, are held in all districts and within temple compounds for, according to popular belief, 'the souls have gone back and it is certain that the Buddha has rescued them from hell and welcomed them into his heaven'. Today, it is customary to end the day with a firework display.

◀ In the days leading up to the *bon* festival, graves are cleaned, watered and decorated with flowers to give the ancestors a worthy welcome.

▼ A geisha sprinkles water on a grave on the day of the ancestors' festival.

Gardens of the dead and fields of sadness

Until the 49th day after death, a soul is assumed to be wandering and it is necessary to water the grave and pray for it. For a certain period the grave consists only of long, narrow funerary tablets in unpainted wood bearing the deceased's posthumous name together with extracts from Buddhist sutras and inscriptions in Sanskrit, the sacred language of original Buddhism. Later they are replaced by a permanent stele in stone, usually shaped like a small pagoda. The 33rd anniversary of the death is marked with particular ceremony because then the soul relinquishes its individual identity and is absorbed into the symbolic spirit of the 'souls of the ancestors'. During this ceremony the name of the deceased is copied on to a collective family tablet; the personal tablet, which hitherto had adorned the domestic altar, is burned or buried at the cemetery. Formerly a budding sprig of Japanese cedar, pine or cypress was often planted, which helped the soul of the deceased to rise skywards and become a bird. If the tree grew green again, it was thought that the deceased had been reincarnated or become a divinity. In some areas a dead person could have two tombs: one where the body was buried and the second as a resting place for the soul. There are still some cemeteries where no body is buried. For example, after the termination of a pregnancy, since the foetus is not buried, a woman can buy a statuette or a small stele and place it in a 'field of sadness' where she can come for reflection. Some temples, such as the Adashino Nembutsu-ji in Kyoto, have thousands of visitors a year who come to pray for the peace of the *mizuko*, the 'water children'.

◀ Funerary tablets in the Kiyomizu-dera temple, Kyoto.

▶ A cemetery with Mount Fuji in the background.

The companion
of dead children

Jizo bosatsu, the Japanese version of the *bodhisattva*
Kshitigarbha, is especially popular in Japan. He appears in
the form of a shaven-headed monk carrying a pilgrim's
staff. He is often seen at crossroads and helps travellers, but
he is worshipped most because of his role as a protector of
children. He is chiefly a companion to those who died young
and whose soul, according to Buddhist teaching, must travel
to the Sai-no-kawara river where it is at the mercy of the
sorceress Shozuka-no-baba. When the parents, devastated
by the loss of their child, neglect their duties and spend their
time visiting the grave, the dead child feels punished and
must build piles of stones on the banks of the infernal river.
He is stripped of his clothing and made to work without
respite under the control of the sorceress, who tells him he
can get to paradise if he builds a tall enough tower – an
impossible task since she and her assistants destroy the piles
as soon as they are built. At this point Jizo arrives, moved
by the harshness of this interminable labour. He drives away
the demons, comforts the children and hides them in his
great sleeves. It is believed that every stone placed with a
prayer before the statue of Jizo lightens the labour of these
children and shortens their penance. To clothe their young
souls, mothers must hang red and white bibs called *yodare
kake* from the statue. Jizo appears in many guises: some
statues show him with a child in his arms. Sometimes he is
even replaced in a temple by a large number of statues of
children wearing hoods and bibs. It was popularly believed
that these statues were alive – in the 18th century one was
even arrested and bound by the police for not protecting a
pedlar sleeping underneath it from being robbed.

▲ Statuette of a child
representing Jizo, to which
prayers for children's souls
are addressed, in the
Zojo-ji temple, Tokyo.

◀ A bound figure of Jizo
in the temple of Nanzo-in
in Kanmachi, in the suburbs
of Tokyo.

ADASHINO, 'field of sadness', a cemetery containing the steles of aborted foetuses or infants who died during delivery.

AIKIDO, 'way of harmony in the energy of the universe', a martial art devised by Ueshiba Morihei in 1931, which aims to develop feelings of harmony and peace by turning an attacker's violence back against them.

AINU, an aboriginal people of northern Japan, now concentrated in the island of Hokkaido.

ANE-SAMA-NINGYO, 'sister-doll', a faceless doll given as an offering to ward off illness.

ANTOKU BUTO, 'dance of darkness', a dance created by the dancer Hijikata Tatsumi. See *buto*.

ARAGOTO, 'rough style', a type of drama and style of make-up created by the actor Ichikawa Danjuro (1660–1704) to play the roles of heroes endowed with superhuman energy. Much appreciated in Edo *kabuki* theatre.

BONSAI, 'planting on a plate,' a miniaturised tree, grown in a pot, whose branches and roots are cut in a special way.

BOKASHIBORI, a technique for shading colours in tattooing.

BUDO, 'martial way', the collective term for the martial arts that combine physical with spiritual discipline.

BUGAKU, a form of dance drama accompanied by *gagaku* music, originating in Tang dynasty China and introduced to the Imperial Japanese Court in the 17th century.

BUNRAKU, puppet theatre – one of the three main forms of traditional Japanese theatre. The large puppets are operated by three handlers masked in black.

BURAKUMIN, 'hamlet people', the section of the population condemned to ostracism and forced to live in designated areas.

BUSHI, samurai, the elite military class that governed Japan from the 12th to the 19th centuries. The word *bushi* (warrior) carries connotations of nobility, while *samurai* means 'he who serves'.

BUSHIDO, 'the warriors' way', the code of honour of the samurai, developed during the Edo period and inspired by the study of Confucianism and the precepts of Zen Buddhism.

BUTO, a form of avant-garde dance of the 1970s, described as 'post-Hiroshima' by critics but often inspired by ancient Japanese folk dancing.

BUTSUDAN, a household altar containing a statue of Buddha and the tablets of ancestors.

BUYO or *nihon-buyo*, Japanese 'classical' dances, including those of the *no* and *kabuki* theatre.

CHIGO, 'small boy', a sacred page supposed to represent the gods during Shinto festivities.

CHUNORI, an actor's acrobatic leap above the stage in *kabuki* theatre.

DO, 'way', the path or discipline needed to reach a goal in a particular art or technique.

EDO, the reign of the Tokugawa *shogun*, from 1603 to 1868, and the ancient name of Tokyo during the same period.

EMA, 'horse's image', a wooden votive tablet, originally showing a horse, offered to Shinto deities in gratitude after a wish is made.

EN, the concept of space based on the tension between the edges of two surfaces, such as that of a veranda between a traditional house and its garden.

ETA, 'the impure ones', the social class consisting of people whose trade is linked to blood or death, considered inferior until its abolition in 1871.

FURIN, a small bronze or porcelain bell whose clapper, moved by the wind, bears a long paper strip adorned with a poem or a prayer.

FUTON, a thin layer used as a mattress, which is unrolled on to a *tatami* mat for the night.

GASSHO, a Buddhist greeting, with the hands joined together as if in prayer.

GEISHA, 'she who excels in the arts', formerly a high-ranking courtesan, the geisha is now a model, expert in the traditional arts, which she demonstrates at evening gatherings of rich or influential men.

GIMU, a person's unavoidable obligations to the state, to parents, and to ancestors.

GIRI, compelling duties or social obligations to the world or to oneself.

GO, a game of strategy, originally from China, played on a gridded board using black and white stones.

GOMA, the ritual symbolic burning of passions during the ceremonies of esoteric Buddhist sects.

HACHIMAKI, a sweatband worn round the head by men during Shinto *matsuri* festivals. Also worn to indicate a vow or commitment.

HAGAKURE, *In the Shade of the Leaves*, a collection of 1,300 commentaries gathered together by Yamamoto Tsunemoto (1659–1719), dealing with the spirit of *bushido*.

HAKADA MATSURI, 'naked festival, a New Year festival in which half-naked young people compete for talismans.

HAKAMA, loose trousers formerly worn by warriors, now worn by practitioners of certain martial arts, *miko* in Shinto shrines, and men in traditional ceremonial garb.

HAMAGURI, a shellfish often depicted to represent the female sex.

HANEBORI, a 'downy' or 'glittering' tattooing technique.

HAORI, a half-length jacket worn over a kimono. It is fastened at the front with a decorative knot and usually bears the family coat of arms.

HARAIGUSHI, a large whip made of paper, used by a Shinto priest to purify the congregation.

HARAKIRI, see *seppuku*.

HARE, used to describe special moments in time, recognised by society and therefore sanctified, such as birth and marriage.

HEIAN, 'Time of peace and tranquillity', the period from 794 to 1185 when the emperor ruled Japan alone. It saw the assimilation of borrowings from Chinese culture on a large scale, and the emergence of a typically Japanese aristocratic culture now considered 'classical'.

HITOBASHIRA, 'human pillar', in the early period of Japanese history a person buried alive to appease the deities of the earth during the construction or consecration of a religious site.

HORIMONO, 'engraved thing' or *irezumi*, a traditional Japanese tattoo.

IKEBANA, a floral arrangement originally conceived as a Buddhist offering, now chiefly a social or educational art, like the tea ceremony.

IREZUMI or *horimono*, a traditional Japanese tattoo.

JIZO BOSATSU, the *bodhisattva* Ksitigarbha, protector of children and travellers.

JOSHI, a double suicide for love. It was fashionable during the Edo period until it was forbidden in 1722.

JUDO, 'way of suppleness', a martial art devised by Kano Jigoro in 1882, based on the fighting techniques of *jujutsu*, and aimed at developing a peaceful state of mind.

JUJUTSU, 'technique of suppleness', an unarmed combat technique.

JUNSHI, suicide to join someone in death. The sacrifice of a servant on the death of his master,

practised especially among warriors. Officially forbidden in 1660.

JUTSU, a 'technique', a method based on traditional teaching; often distinguished from 'the way', *do*, in martial arts.

KABUKI ODORI, extravagant dances invented by the female dancer Okuni in about 1603, which gave rise to *kabuki* theatre.

KABUKI, one of the three main types of Japanese theatre, acted exclusively by men. Aimed at the urban masses, it presents popular heroes in an expressionist style of acting, singing and dancing.

KABUKU, 'to dress in an extravagant manner', the probable origin of the word *kabuki*.

KAGURA, a sacred Shinto dance whose origins date back, according to the *Koji-ki*, the *Records of Ancient Matters*, to the time of the divinities, when the goddess Uzume invented its steps in order to persuade the sun goddess to come out of hiding.

KAISHAKUNIN, a second person whose job it is to decapitate someone committing *seppuku*, once the first cut has been made.

KAMAKURA, the period between 1192 and 1336, when the *shogun* warrior class usurped the power of the emperor, leaving him only a religious and honorary role.

KAMI, 'that which is above', divinities of the Shinto religion. There are several types, including the *kami* of the heavens such as the sun goddess or certain great men who have been deified, but the majority are nature spirits, which must be pacified by means of offerings.

KAMIKAZE, 'divine winds', the name given to the young pilots of suicide aircraft during the Second World War, in memory of the typhoon that wrecked the Mongol fleet which was about to invade Japan in the 13th century.

KAN-MAIRI, a night walk and purification rite carried out in winter by members of the Nichiren Buddhist sect.

KANSHI, a protest suicide by a samurai to draw attention to an injustice or violation of the code of honour.

KARAOKE, 'empty orchestra', a recording of a musical score and video to be used as an accompaniment for an amateur singer. Also used to denote places that offer this form of entertainment.

KARATE, 'empty hands', a system of unarmed combat based on ancient styles of self-defence, developed by the inhabitants of Okinawa for use against the Japanese invaders. It was codified into a martial art, *karate-do*, by Funakoshi Gichin (1869–1957).

KARIGANE, 'wild goose', setting the hair in a 'V' shape in the middle of the forehead, regarded as the acme of beauty.

KATA 'form', theoretical movements that aim to achieve excellence in the execution of techniques such as those of *no* and *kabuki* theatre, craftsmanship and martial arts.

KE, the interval between two *hare* moments, as related to events of everyday life rather than rites and religious ceremonies.

KEGARE, the concept of ritual purity and impurity, formerly associated with the idea of crime and sin which required purification.

KENDO, 'way of the sword', a martial art that involves training in handling a sword. It is practised using a sword with a bamboo blade, and light armour.

KESA, Buddhist garment covering the right shoulder and passing beneath the left arm. Simplified to a sack shape in Zen work clothes.

KIAKE, gift offered by the family of a dead person to all those who have made an offering to the deceased's spirit, and to those who have helped with the funeral rites.

KIMONO, 'thing to be worn', a set of Japanese, as opposed to Western, clothing. Most often used to denote women's clothes and the dress of martial arts practitioners.

KONA-O-SHIROI, a white powder used to give a matt finish. It is laid over the *neri-o-shiroi*.

KOYA SAN, Mount Koya, in the centre of the Kii peninsula, where Kukai founded the principal temple of the Shingon sect. Famous for its necropolis.

KUMADORI, the highly expressive make-up used in *kabuki*, which conveys the role and personality of the characters.

KYOGEN, a comic interlude, developed from ancient pantomimes, between two *no* scenes.

KYOSAKU, the rod used by a monk to 'awaken' the attention of the practitioner during the seated meditation of *zazen*.

LOLIKON, 'Lolita complex', attraction for, and fantasies about, young girls.

MA, the concept of space or emptiness between two successive events. Used in the arts, painting, drama, music, dance and martial arts to define an interval.

MAIKO, an apprentice geisha practising dance, music and good manners while welcoming a guest.

MANGA, comic drawings or caricatures of very ancient origin. Particularly vigorous during the Edo period, today these 'sketches' have been transformed into graphic novels and animated films.

MATSURI, Shinto festival in honour of a local divinity, and seasonal rites. Some *matsuri* have become purely commercial festivals.

MEIJI, the period of the Meiji emperor's reign, from 1868 to 1912.

MIE, 'blinding image', an exaggerated pose in *kabuki*, adopted by an actor to show off his talent.

MIKO, originally shamans who, in a trance, could communicate with the *kami* and the souls of the dead, and were entrusted with carrying out rites such as the *kagura*. Today *miko* are young girls in the service of the divinity of a Shinto shrine, which they petition and make offerings to in their dances.

MIKOSHI, a sacred Shinto palanquin, the temporary residence of a divinity.

MISOGI, purification with water, typical of Shinto rites, ranging from bathing the hands and mouth to total immersion in the sea or in a waterfall.

MIYAKO ODORI, dance performances by the geisha and *maiko* of Kyoto.

MIZU-AGE, the ceremony of the deflowering of a *maiko*.

MIZUGORI, a *misogi* using iced water.

MIZUKO, 'child of the water', an aborted foetus.

MUROMACHI, an artistic and historical period under the Ashikaga *shogun*, from 1366 to 1568.

NAGASHI-BINA, 'dolls left to drift', purification dolls credited with carrying away impurities and illnesses with the current.

NAKODO, a person in charge of arranging marriages and acting as an intermediary between the families of future married couples.

NAORAI, Shinto right of communion between the *kami* and the faithful, carried out at a banquet when food and *sake* are offered to divinities.

NEBUTA, huge lanterns used during festivals such as the Aomori *nebuta matsuri*.

NERI-O-SHIROI, a non-metallic white make-up which replaced white lead in about 1880.

NO, one of the three main types of traditional Japanese theatre, acted exclusively by men.

Aimed at the warrior class, it presents legendary heroes of past centuries. The leading actors, who play supernatural characters or women, wear masks.

O-BON or *urabon*, a 'festival of souls', a Buddhist festival held in mid-July. Over three days, ancestors are invited to return to their former dwelling to receive the affection of their descendants.

O-HARAI, 'great purification', a solemn ceremony held in Shinto shrines.

OBI, a broad belt for keeping a kimono closed. Those worn by men and elderly people are narrower; the shape of the knot varies according to age and social status.

OBIAGE, a soft scarf that acts as padding behind the knot in an *obi*. It protrudes over the front of the belt to varying degrees, according to a woman's age.

ODORI, or *asobi*, or *mai*, ancient folk dances. Those performed by geisha and in *miyako-odori* belong to this type.

OIRAN, a high-ranking geisha title.

ONNAGATA, a man playing a female role in *kabuki* theatre.

ORIGAMI, 'folded paper', the art of folding paper; originally religious and ritual, later ceremonial, and finally a pastime.

PACHINKO, a kind of vertical Japanese pinball machine.

POKKURI, raised clogs worn by *maiko*, in lacquered or carved wood, secured to the feet by thongs between the big toe and the other toes.

SAIKEIREI, the most respectful form of greeting.

SAILOR FUKU, the 'sailor' uniform worn by secondary school girls.

SAKAKI, *cleyera ochnacea*, the sacred tree of Shinto, whose branches are often used in rites.

SAKE, an alcoholic drink made from fermented rice.

SAMBON-ASHI, 'three legs', three pointed areas on the back of a geisha's neck where make-up is not applied. 'Two legs' make-up is reserved for *maiko*.

SAMURAI, see *bushi*.

SANSANKUDO, 'three times three is nine', part of a marriage ceremony, in which the newlyweds exchange three cups of *sake*, each of which they must drink in three draughts to seal their union.

SATORI, the Buddhist 'awakening' – a fundamental concept of Zen Buddhism. This state of enlightenment, innate in every being, is attainable either suddenly or gradually, depending on the sect.

SENKAJI FUDA, 'papers of the thousand temples', pieces of paper stuck to the wooden framework of temples by the faithful when they come to pray for the realisation of a wish or the health of a friend.

SENTO, a public bath.

SEPPUKU, popularly known as *hara-kiri*: a warrior's ritual suicide by disembowelment as a result of defeat or dishonour, to accompany his lord in death or to express his disapproval.

SHAMISEN, a type of three-stringed lute used by *kabuki* and puppet theatre musicians, as well as by geisha.

SHI, 'four', an unlucky number for living people as it sounds the same as the word for death. The pronunciation *yon* is preferred for this reason.

SHICHI-GO-SAN, the festival of children aged 'seven, five and three', held to bring divine grace upon them.

SHIMADA, the knot of hair worn by courtesans in the Edo period, now only worn by geisha. A more elaborate version is worn by brides in traditional dress.

SHINGON, 'true word', esoteric Buddhist sect introduced from China by the monk Kukai at the beginning of the ninth century. Its principal monastery is on Mount Koya.

SHINTO, indigenous religion of Japan, involving the worship of thousands of spirits in nature and many purification rites. In the course of Japan's history, Shinto and Buddhism were often associated by various processes of fusion, until Shinto became the state religion during the Meiji period.

SHIRABYOSHI, temple dances invented during the 12th century and performed during certain Buddhist ceremonies. The same name is given to the female dancers themselves, who often wear a man's robe and hat, and carry a sword.

SHITE, 'he who takes action', the leading actor in *no* plays. He is generally masked.

SHOGUN, a kind of military dictator who monopolised all powers, leaving the emperor only a religious and honorary role. The *shogun* governed Japan from 1192 to 1868.

SHUGENDO, a collective term for the esoteric religious sects that practise asceticism as a means of revealing to their practitioners, the *yamabushi*, the true nature of their enlightenment.

SUMO, ritual combat of Shinto origin that pits two wrestlers, *sumotori*, against each other in a circular arena symbolising the heavens. The contest is preceded by ritual exorcism and purification using salt.

TABI, two-toed socks designed to be worn with traditional shoes and kimono.

TAKENOKO, 'young bamboo shoots', a term used for adolescents who go dancing at the weekend in Yoyogi Park, Tokyo.

TATAMI, mats made from compressed rice straw, the size of a recumbent man, that cover the floor of traditionally furnished rooms.

TAYU, a high-ranking geisha title.

TOKONOMA, in traditional architecture, a shallow alcove in the principal room containing works of art, calligraphy, painting, a censer and *ikebana*.

TSURU, the crowned crane, the bird that symbolises Japan. Very often represented in art and paper folding.

UBU-GI, the ceremonial dress worn by a child on his or her first presentation to the Shinto gods.

URA, the 'reverse' or 'underside', the hidden world.

WAKI, 'he who is beside', the actor playing the second most important role in *no* after the *shite*.

YAKUZA, 'eight-nine-three', a Japanese gangster, whose name comes from the losing combination in a game. Organised into vast 'families', the *yakuza* focus their activities on the gambling and sex industries.

YAKYU, Japanese for baseball.

YAMABUSHI, 'he who sleeps on the mountain', a monk who practises asceticism, magic, divination and walking on fire.

YODARE KAKE, red and white bibs given as offerings to the statues of Jizo.

YUGEN, 'subtle grace', an aesthetic concept that aims to give things an appearance of mystery, elegance and measured sadness.

YUKATA, 'bathrobe', a light cotton kimono usually worn after a bath in summer, for relaxing in or for dancing during a *matsuri*.

ZAZEN, a seated posture in Zen meditation, which aims to achieve the emptiness of enlightenment.

ZEN, meditation, from the Sanskrit *dhyana*. A school of Buddhism which demands that the practitioner achieve *satori* through mental concentration or the study of 'paradoxes'. Japanese Zen consists of three main sects: Soto, Rinzai and Obaku.

BIBLIOGRAPHY

AUBERT, LOUIS, *Paix japonaise*, Colin, Paris, 1906.

BABA, AKIKO, *Horreur et Pureté*, East-Orient, vol. 1, Tokyo, 1967.

BARTHES, ROLAND, *L'Empire des signes*, Albert Skira, Geneva, 1970.

BEFU, HARUMI, *Japan, an anthropological introduction*, Chandler Publishing Co, New York, 1971.

BENEDICT, RUTH, *Le Chrysanthème et le sabre*, Éditions Piquier, Paris, 1987.

BERQUE, AUGUSTIN, *Vivre l'espace du Japon*, Presses Universitaires de France, Paris, 1982.

BERQUE, AUGUSTIN, *Le Sauvage et l'artifice, Les Japonais devant la nature*, Gallimard, Paris, 1986.

BERQUE, AUGUSTIN (ed.), *Dictionnaire de la civilisation japonaise*, Hazan, Paris, 1994.

CHALLAYE, FELICIEN, *Le Japon illustré*, Librairie Larousse, Paris, 1915.

CHAMBERLAIN, BASIL, *Moeurs et coutumes du Japon*, Payot, Paris, 1931.

COYAU, MAURICE, *Fêtes au Japon*, PAF, 1978.

DELAY, NELLY, *L'Estampe japonaise*, Hazan, Paris, 1993.

DURSTON, DIANE, *Japan Crafts Sourcebook*, Kodansha International, 1996.

ELISSEEFF, DANIELLE, *Les Dames du Soleil levant*, Stock-L Pernoud, Paris, 1993.

FREDERIC, LOUIS, *La Vie quotidienne au Japon à l'époque des samourais*, Hachette, Paris, 1984.

FREDERIC, LOUIS, *La Vie quotidienne au Japon au début de l'ère moderne*, Hachette, Paris, 1984.

FREDERIC, LOUIS, *Le Japon, dictionnaire et civilisation*, Robert Laffont, 'Bouquins' collection, Paris, 1996.

GUILLAIN, ROBERT, *Les Geishas*, Arléa, Paris, 1988.

HEARN, LAFCADIO, *Japan, An Attempt at Interpretation*, Macmillan, New York, 1984.

HOSHINO, KOMARO, *Ukiyoe kuzushi*, NGS, Tokyo, 1981.

IMMOOS, THOMAS, *Théâtre japonais*, Les Éditions de Bonvent, Geneva, 1974.

JAPAN PHOTOGRAPHERS' ASSOCIATION, *A Century of Japanese Photography*, Hutchinson, Auckland, 1971.

JAPAN TRAVEL BUREAU, *Festivals of Japan*, 1985.

KONDO, AKIHISA, *Derrière le masque*, East-Orient, vol. 1, Tokyo, 1967.

KOREN, LEONARD, *Mode au Japon*, Herscher, Paris, 1985.

KOZAIKAI, TOSHIAKI, 'Le Blanc d'honneur' in *Ovni*, No. 1333, 15 March 1989.

LOTI, PIERRE, *Mukashi, mukashi*, Arthaud, Paris, 1984.

MARQUIS DE LA MAZELIERE, *Histoire et Civilisation*, Plon, Paris, 1907.

MARTRES, LAURENT, *Sumo, le sport et le sacré*, Graphie International, Inc.

MAYBON, ALBERT, *Le Théâtre japonais*, Henri Laurens Éditions, 1925.

MISHIMA, YUKIO, *Le Japon moderne et l'éthique samourai*, translated from the English by Émile Jean, Gallimard, 'Arcades' collection, Paris, 1985.

MIYAKE, ISSEY, *East meets West*, Heibonsha, Tokyo, 1978.

MORRIS, IVAN, *La Noblesse de l'échec, héros tragiques de l'histoire du Japon*, Gallimard, Paris, 1980.

MORSE, EDWARD, *Japanese Homes and Their Surroundings*, Harper & Franklin, New York, 1895.

KWOK ON MUSEUM, *Fêtes traditionnelles en Asie, Japon*, 1984.

MUSICAL, 'Le kabuki' in *Revue du Théâtre musical de Paris-Châtelet*, 1987.

NAKANE, CHIE, *La Société japonaise*, Armand Colin, Paris, 1967.

OHARA, REIKO, *Revue d'esthétique, Japon*, Éditions Jean Michel Place, Paris, 1990.

PINGUET, MAURICE, *La Mort volontaire au Japon*, Gallimard, Paris, 1984.

RANDOM, MICHEL, *Japon, la stratégie de l'invisible*, Éditions du Félin, Paris, 1985.

REVON, MICHEL, *Anthologie de la littérature Japonaise*, Librairie Ch. Delagrave, Paris, 1910.

SABOURET, JEAN-FRANCOIS, *L'État du Japon*, La Découverte, Paris, 1988.

SHIBATA, MARUMI and MARYSE, *Kojiki*, Maisonneuve et Larose, Paris 1969.

SIEFFERT, RENE, *La Tradition secrète du nô*, Gallimard-Unesco, Paris, 1960.

SUZUKI, SHUNRYU, *Esprit zen, esprit neuf*, Editions du Seuil, Paris, 1977.

TANIZAKI, JUNICHIRO, *Éloge de l'ombre*, translated by René Sieffert, Presses Orientalistes de France, Paris, 1977.

TANIZAKI, JUNICHIRO, *Le Tatouage*, translated by Madeleine Levy.

TESSIER, MAX, *Images du cinéma japonais*, Henri Veyrier, Paris, 1990.

TOKYO ASAHI SHIMBUN, *Changing Japan Seen Through the Camera*, 1933.

'Japon fiction' in *Traverses*, Nos 38–9, Revue du Centre Georges-Pompidou, Paris, 1986.

TSUDA, ITSUO, *Le Non-faire, école de la respiration*, Le courrier du Livre, Paris, 1973.

YAMAGUCHI, M and KOJIMA, S, *A Cultural Dictionary of Japan*, The Japan Times, 1985.

YAMAGUCHI, MASAO, 'Le maquillage traditionnel au Japon' in *Traverses* No. 7, Éditions de Minuit, Paris, 1976.

YAMANAKA, KEIKO, *L'Archipel écartelé*, Tsuru Éditions, 1990.

YOSHIDA, MITSUKUNI, *Harmony with Nature*, Cosmo Public Relations Corp, Tokyo, 1986.

YOSHIDA, MITSUKUNI, *The People's Culture from Kyoto to Edo*, Cosmo Public Relations Corp, Tokyo, 1986.

YOSHIDA, MITSUKUNI, *Asobi*, Cosmo Public Relations Corp, Tokyo, 1987.

BY THE SAME AUTHOR:

– *Temples et sanctuaries au Japon*, Éditions du Moniteur, Paris, 1980.

– *Kimono, art traditionnel du Japon*, Edita/La Bibliothèque des Arts, Lausanne, 1983.

– *Regards sur la femme japonaise*, text only, photographs by Natacha Hochman, Éditions Hatier-Perron, 1985.

– *La Vie et l'oeuvre de Léonard Tsuguharu Foujita*, with Sylvie Buisson, Édition ACR, Courbevoie, 1987.

– *Le Chat vu par les peintres. Inde, Corée, Chine*, Edita, Lausanne/Vilo, 1988.

– *Manuel pratique d'origami*, Édition Arted, 1988.

– *Papiers plies, des idées plain les mains*, J'ai lu, Paris, 1989.

– *Architectures sacrées du Japon*, Éditions ACR, Courbevoie, 1989.

– *Japon-Papier*, Finest SA/Éditions Pierre Terrail, 1991.

– 'Le design' and 'La mode', entries in *Dictionnaire du Japon contemporain*, Hazan, Paris, 1994.

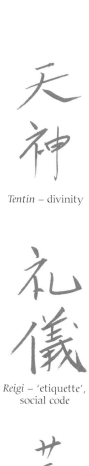

天神

Tentin – divinity

職人

Shokunin – craftsman

礼儀

Reigi – 'etiquette',
social code

祭典

Saiten – festivity

芸者

Geisha

能面

Nomen – *no* mask

化粧

Kesho – make-up

空間

Kukan – space–time

武士

Bushi – samurai

地蔵

Jizo

ACKNOWLEDGEMENTS

The author would like to thank the following for their help and advice: Ariadone-buto, the Sakaide Studio in Gifu, Akira and Takashi Buseki, Mr and Mrs Fukumoto, Ichikawa Ennosuke III, Shozo Iida, Carlotta Ikeda, Atsuko Inobe, Junko Inobe, Mitsuru Isezaki, Shinichiro Ishii, Bernard Jeannel, Kabuki-za, Tokyo, Hitoshi Kadoi, Magoroku Kaneko, Marc Peter Keane, Ryo and Hiromi Kinoshita, Kazuo Kobayashi, Machi Kojima, Takashi and Chie Kuroda, Junko Kusunoki, Jiko Kyodo, Madeleine Lévy, Hélène and Jean Lühl, Chie Maingard-Yuhara, Noriko and Yoshimi Maruyama, Hiroshi Matsuyama, Issey Miyake, Reiko and Shinichi Nadai, Yasue Nakai, Masanori Nishimura, Morio Nishio, Minosuke Oe, Megumi Onoda, Izumi Oshima, Sennya Sakurai, Yoshikata Sasai, Yoshioka Sashio, Masao Sato, Claude Saulière, Tsuyu Shimizu, the Shozan Company, Kyoto, the Sochiku Company, Eiji Sugimoto, Masu Suzuki, Shigeru Taga, Mami Takahashi, Min Tanaka, the Toei Film Company, Sesoko Tsune, Masaru Umazume, Mari Watanabe, Rumiko Yamasaki, Noriko Yasue.

The author would especially like to thank Tsuyu, Rumiko, Kazumi, Yasue, Chie and Tsunemaru for appearing in this book, Masako Saulière for calligraphy, the Vandystadt Agency for its courtesy and collaboration with photography, Pleats Please, Véronique Vasseur, and Francis Giacobetti for photographs of recent collections by Issey Miyake, and especially Marie-France Schaeffer for her help and daily support.

Photographs and documents in this book are by the author with the exception of the photographs on pages:
© Pleats Please, photo Francis Giacobetti: pp 124, 126–7.
© Max Tessier: p 82.
© Gérard Vandystadt: Agence Vandystadt, Paris: pp 14–15, 32 (bottom), 146.

First published by Hazan, an imprint of Hachette-Livre
43 Quai de Grenelle, Paris 75905, Cedex 15, France
© Dominique Buisson
Under the title Le Corps Japonais

Language translation produced by Translate-A-Book, Oxford
Typesetting by Organ Graphic, Abingdon

© 2003 English translation, Octopus Publishing Group Ltd, London
This edition published by Hachette Illustrated UK, Octopus Publishing Group,
2–4 Heron Quays, London, E14 4JP

Printed by Tien Wah, Singapore
ISBN: 1-84430-028-5